Roses are Red

SURVIVAL & RECOVERY
BY GOD'S GRACE

a true story by
Rose Anne Daniels

Roses are Red

Tate Publishing & *Enterprises*

Roses Are Red
Copyright © 2008 by Rose Anne Daniels. All rights reserved.

This title is also available as a Tate Out Loud product. Visit www.tatepublishing.com for more information.

No part of this publication may be reproduced, stored in a retrieval system or transmitted in any way by any means, electronic, mechanical, photocopy, recording or otherwise without the prior permission of the author except as provided by USA copyright law.

The opinions expressed by the author are not necessarily those of Tate Publishing, LLC.

Published by Tate Publishing & Enterprises, LLC
127 E. Trade Center Terrace | Mustang, Oklahoma 73064 USA
1.888.361.9473 | www.tatepublishing.com

Tate Publishing is committed to excellence in the publishing industry. The company reflects the philosophy established by the founders, based on Psalm 68:11,
"The Lord gave the word and great was the company of those who published it."

Book design copyright © 2008 by Tate Publishing, LLC. All rights reserved.
Cover design by Lindsay B. Behrens
Interior design by Joey Garrett

Published in the United States of America

ISBN: 978-1-60604-786-6
1. Autobiography, Bipolar Disorder
2. Health, Christian Living, Suffering
08.08.02

To the Almighty God who created me for such a unique
purpose, who sustained and delivered me from all my trials

To health care workers, family, and friends
who endured with me, often at wit's end

To my children who never stopped believing in me

To my grandchildren who have
caused me to forget the pain

Table of Contents

13	A Career
17	Beginnings
23	An Introduction / A Calling
27	Success
35	Security
39	A Drug-Enforced Haven
43	A Mountain to Climb
47	Failure
55	It Only Seems Like More Than I Can Endure
61	Survival
69	Grace
77	More Grace
81	On My Own

91	A New Definition of Security
97	God's Helpers
103	A New Definition of Success
107	Forgiveness Is Not Necessarily Reconciliation
111	A New Direction
113	Wholeness
117	Endnotes

Foreword

Dear Rose,

    Your life-history has been on my mind for over a month now and I haven't forgotten your request that I write an introduction.

    The thought that comes again and again to me, is that I never dreamed you had been through such a struggle! I saw in you a lovely young woman and I filled in an imaginary past: a southern home, a gentle and gracious family, protecting their daughter from the harsh aspects of life, and bringing her up with the gracious manners and charm of the southern culture.

    The story of your past, your experience of the terrifying ups and downs of the bipolar affliction, and the fearful isolation in which you had to combat it, made me realize that my earlier view of your personality was almost all the work of my imagination. Almost, but not entirely, for in your healing you had experienced the Grace of God. It was this grace in which I saw in you, healing the wounds of the past, and supplying the love that shone in your presence and manner.

Reading the story of your life, I was gripped by the terrors of your affliction and in your final victory I experienced anew our savior's promise that He has overcome the world, and that He saves to the uttermost!

These thoughts are very real to me, and I want you to know how deep into my heart you reached in telling your story!

Your friend as ever,
Reverend Thomas Charles

> I am the rose of Sharon, The lily of the valleys.
>
> Song of Solomon 2:1

> Get yourself up on a high mountain, O Zion, bearer of good news, Lift up your voice mightily, O Jerusalem, bearer of good news; Lift *it* up, do not fear. Say to the cities of Judah, "Here is your God!"
>
> Isaiah 40:9

Our knowledge of Christ is somewhat like climbing one of the mountains in Wales. When you are at the base you see only a little: the mountain itself appears to be only half as high as it really is. Confined in a little valley, you discover scarcely anything but the rippling brooks as they descend into the stream at the foot of the mountain. Climb the first rising knoll, and the valley lengthens and widens beneath your feet. Go higher, and you see the country for four or five miles around, and you are delighted with the widening prospect. Higher still, and the scene enlarges; until at last, when you are on the summit and look east, west, north, south, you see almost all of England lying before you. There is a forest in some distant county, perhaps two hundred miles away, and here the sea, and there a shining river and the smoking chimneys of a manufacturing town, or the mast of the ships in a busy port. All these things please and delight you, and you say, "I could not have imagined that so much could be seen at this elevation." Now, the Christian life is of the same order. When we first believe in Christ, we see only a little of Him. The higher we climb, the more we discover of His beauty. But who has ever gained the summit? Who has known all the heights and depths of the love of Christ that passes knowledge?[1]

    Charles H. Spurgeon, *Morning and Evening*

A Career

Dedication to family was first and foremost in the culture I grew up in. Never in my sleepy daydreaming times of early youth did I imagine myself as anything other than a devoted wife who cooked home-style meals surrounded by no fewer than six contented children. It was first made apparent to me that there was another slant on this picture by my guidance counselor in eighth grade. Mrs. Jordan looked seriously at my grades and announced that I would be taking college preparatory classes in high school. I sat straight up from my slumped position to hear this announcement. My parents and grandparents had not attended college and, although one uncle had graduated from veterinary school, my parents had nothing good to say about him. My family had ostracized him, as he was no longer a member of the community or the country church my family attended. I remember the words spoken by my father and older brother: "book learnin' don't mean nothin.'" I was use to doing as I was told and this meeting was a crossroad of my life. To pursue the path my teachers had put me on was at odds with the path of my family. I wondered if I would be considered "snooty."

I had an A minus average in school. My parents would look at my report card with all the enthusiasm of sailors drowning at sea. I was aware that my grades were neither a concern nor an accomplishment. The only comment that I remember on one occasion came from my mother: "why the minus?" My father's glance at my grades seemed to wound him. I remember seriously considering flunking a class just to see what the reaction would be. At this point in my life my good sense overruled my need for attention and I abandoned the thought. Besides, I had plenty of attention at school.

Where could my grades take me? I approached the problem as if there were no limits and, financial situation aside, I decided I would be a medical social worker requiring a master's degree. My keenest desire since childhood, other than family security, was to join the Peace Corps. I had written them a letter when I was twelve offering my services. The reply was gracious although eye-opening: they most needed medical people, including registered nurses.

I was looking for something that was within my reach. I found two federally-assisted diploma registered nurse programs within driving distance. One of them was a twenty-four month program; the other program was thirty-three months in length. The first nine months required college courses at nearby colleges, and the remainder of the courses were taught at hospitals. Employment as nursing assistants was allowed. Nursing offered different shifts, part-time employment, and many opportunities. I pictured structuring my life around a husband and six children after all.

Shortly after I made this decision, my Girl Scout troop offered an explorer program that allowed me to take a position as a candy striper. My first evening at our local hospital, still adjusting to ever-present odors, gaping wounds, and the semi-nudity of open-backed gowns, the nurses sent me to the delivery room to witness a birth. I was a bit tardy after gowning and gloving for the event. In fact, I missed the delivery of the child entirely and arrived just in time to see the delivery of the placenta. I passed out.

Getting up from the floor I made a mental note that I might have to rule out certain types of nursing and pursue others. Little did I know at the time that my career would be characterized by getting up from the floor.

The following summer I took a job as a nurse's aide at the same hospital and I came to know the women I worked with and to admire them greatly. They were the epitome of calm in the storms of life. They both laughed and cried with their patients. They faced the uncertain, the unpredictable, and the unfair with grace, dignity, and professionalism. I was determined to put my heart and soul into the pursuit of a dream to be like them.

My senior year I applied and was accepted at the nursing school of my choice. In addition to the other requirements for admission I had to take a psychological test. This intrigued me as I wondered what the school was looking for but, after my acceptance, I smiled with the realization that they were looking for someone just like me.

As I look at my all-class high school graduation picture I see that no one was beaming any brighter than I was. My smile reflected my satisfaction at having chosen a path and being on that path.

Beginnings

My childhood would not be colored with a full box of crayons. The colors I most remember are orange, black, and purple. To me, purple has always stood for majesty, much like the vestments the priest wore during the Mass. It was so contrasted with the colors of Halloween as to be all the more obvious. This is the advantage that I had.

I was born into rural mid America in the fifties. My parents were from farming heritage, and they bought one hundred acres of land shortly before I was born. I was the second child and the first daughter. I will not say that I was unwanted, but I was unplanned. Being second-born colored my childhood. Girls were not chosen to learn Latin to be altar servers. I was taught that I was only allowed on the altar with a vacuum cleaner.

There was much unsaid in my family. Communication between family members was usually conducted behind closed doors. I could not go to my parents with problems since the standard answer I would receive was "you think you have problems *now* . . . just wait until you are older." I often felt the words spoken over me and my siblings to be curses rather than blessings. I remember not wanting to grow up at all.

The words I most remember being directed at me were "selfish" and "lazy." The labels hung over me like dark clouds threatening to produce the whirlwind that would destroy any future I might dream of. They were spoken by my mother when she was in one of her dark moods that she was determined she did not need help for. Later she would appear at my bedside when the mood would lift and tearfully beg my forgiveness because she was "a terrible mother." I always forgave her. The pleadings for forgiveness would become less frequent and disappear altogether as I grew older. My father would leave when these moods appeared. She would scream, "Just leave then!" and he would retort "Kathy, you are full of the devil!" The solutions to the problem were as unchanging as the problem itself. I would retreat to a rocking chair in the corner as the security I needed in lieu of the hugs that were missing in my home.

The house we lived in was a country house that had been converted from a chicken house. This was discovered when attempting to add on a living room and feathers began flying from the roof. I was sick frequently with respiratory illness that would later be identified at my school as histoplasmosis, which could be attributable to playing in soil rich with chicken dung. On one occasion a snake entered the house during a heavy rain and slithered down the wall behind the couch. I don't remember that we ever found it. The house was too small for what would eventually be a family of seven. My parents believed that to allow a child to grow up in the country was to give that child every advantage, and priority was therefore given to acreage and not the living situation.

We were somewhat isolated from our neighbors, although

we faithfully attended Mass in a nearby country town every Sunday. The "town" consisted of one gas station, one general store, two school buildings, one church, and a cemetery. Visits to my grandparents usually followed. My maternal grandmother supplied the love that was missing in my home. Still, she was labeled by several in my father's family as "a strange woman" because she would not leave her home and go out in public. Even a trip to the grocery store was more than she could bear. She limited her social life to her family, and she did not drive a car. Her relationship with my maternal grandfather was resigned tolerance as they had separate bedrooms, but she still cooked his meals and submitted to his choices. What I remember most about her is that she seemed to take delight in me as a child, without any reserve. My grandfather had an estranged relationship with my mother and he refused to attend the wedding between my parents. He agreed to pay for her psychiatric hospitalization when it became obvious that she needed help. My mother made sure that it was never obvious again.

I was six when I started first grade in the nearby country school. Mrs. Jones was very strict. She had ten first graders who had never attended kindergarten, rarely worked a puzzle, and seldom traveled more that a ten-mile radius. Her first rule of order was to instill a strict code of discipline, in itself no small task. I don't remember being spanked but I was engrossed in watching the punishment when someone else was so unfortunate as to deserve her sentencing. In fact, *no one* in the class was going to do *that* again.

The next dilemma was the need for a paradigm shift. Mrs. Jones wanted to convert our young minds from "I can speak and be understood" to the much more prosperous "I have to speak correctly to get what I need." Apparently she had discovered what I considered "the bathroom game" to be the most effective method to achieve the desired result. We had to raise our hand to ask to go to the bathroom. When called upon we were all so unknowing as to ask the same question, "Can I go to the bathroom?" Mrs. Jones would calmly say "You *can* go to the bathroom, but the question you need to ask is "*May* I go to the bathroom?" Focusing only on the first part of her answer the somewhat perplexed student would get up to go to the bathroom. This action would be met with Mrs. Jones' ire while she nearly shouted, "You haven't asked for *permission* to go the bathroom!" Completely perplexed, the student would lamely reply "But you said 'you can go to the bathroom.'" The game continued until everyone got it right.

We were taught phonics to read. By the time I could read I remember having one specific puzzle at home, a puzzle of the United States with names of the states printed on each. One day Mrs. Jones stood in front of the class and asked if anyone knew names of the states. Quite certain I had been given a moment to shine I confidently pointed out the easy-to-sound-out states. Mrs. Jones was all aglow until I tried to locate Igan. She shook her head and was quite certain there wasn't a state by that name. I was equally certain and loudly adamant that there was, indeed, an Igan, and I pointed to its location. She tried to suppress the grin, as I recall, although it must have been too much for her as she realized that Michigan had a lake that divided my puzzle into Mich and Igan.

Mrs. Jones was my teacher for first and second grade. What I remember most about her were the words she spoke frequently over me. They were a blessing that I clung to: "Rose will always do well in school."

My best friends were from families larger than mine. Becky was eleventh of thirteen children; Connie was ninth of eleven; and Jo Ellen was eighth of thirteen. We giggled and played as little girls do on the hour-long bus ride home from school. My brothers and sisters and I were fortunate to be "last" on the country run which meant we were the last to be picked-up in the morning.

Our church was next to the school and, sometimes, we attended Mass before school. This was not required but often suggested strongly as the entire community was Catholic except for one divorced mother with only two children who were often gossiped about.

The summer of my seventh year was a turning point in my life. Daniel, a young priest who had not yet been ordained came to our community to teach catechism. I remember him as a smiling, enthusiastic, lover of children who stood in bold contrast to the regular priest of our parish. Our priest, who boomed from the lectern in a fierce voice the certainties of hell fires if commandments were broken, had once roared at Jo Ellen and me "Get thee behind me Satan!" as we entered the sanctuary unaware that the wind had blown the required chapel veils from our heads on a particularly blustery day. I remember our shamed retreat to the back of the church to pin Kleenex on our heads as a substitute. Oddly, I have no recollection of his face, only of his voice. The rumor, when he suddenly left our church after his housekeeper became pregnant, was that he had been admitted to a psychiatric facility.

Daniel told us to call him "Daniel." He stood in front of a combined class of first and second graders and asked us our names. As my friend introduced herself as "Jo Ellen" I had decided to be equally special and, for the first time, I used my middle name. "I am Rose Anne." My brother, a year older, loudly protested "Her name is just Rose!" But Daniel wisely sensed my need for recognition and, for at least six weeks, I became "Rose Anne."

I vividly recall the first recess when Daniel actually joined our circle of little girls playing "ring around the rosy." As he taught us about our need for a personal relationship with Jesus I was suddenly struck with the realization that Jesus would actually join the little girls playing "ring around the rosy."

The second graders were to receive their first communion at the end of the summer in a ceremony that was to be celebrated with white suits for the boys and white dresses for the girls. It was to be outside this year, a special touch arranged by Daniel. One day he announced that there were three first graders who were ready to receive communion and he felt they should not be held back. I was thrilled to be one of those chosen.

On the day of my seventh birthday Daniel stood in front of the class and announced that "Someone has a birthday!" After the class had sung me "Happy Birthday" he slyly called me into an adjoining room where the class could not watch. As he winked at me he clapped his hands together seven times, loudly, imitating the spank, to the noisy delight of the class. He handed me two shiny quarters that, to me, represented all the money I would ever need in this world.

I took my first communion solemnly as only a child who has learned the preciousness of our Savior can do. When the ceremony was over Daniel would be leaving. He took me aside and gave me a picture of himself and, on the back, he wrote "To Rose Anne" and signed his name. His final words were written "Love Jesus Always."

I would carry this picture in my wallet until my thirties when I would lose it after being committed to a psychiatric hospital.

An Introduction
A Calling

I was seven years old when I developed both pneumonia and measles. I was not an easy patient to care for. My mother had three other children at home, the youngest an infant, and it was my father who took me to the hospital when my temperature climbed to one hundred six degrees. When he left to return to work I sensed that he felt badly about the situation.

I was put in isolation, and I was rebellious as only a lonely child is capable. I was *not* going to use a bedpan. Over the bedrails, with all the strength I could muster, I made it to the bathroom and pulled the cord to see just what an *emergency* was. The entire pediatric ward responded. Rewarded for my behavior, I repeated my antics more than once.

Having recently seen the movie *Bambi*, I dreamed that I was Bambi and all the animals in the forest were chasing me. It was a recurrent nightmare.

I begged for a rocking chair. If only I could be allowed to be out of the bed to rock in a chair, I would be good, I pleaded. One day my doctor, with a very kind smile, produced the rocking chair. True to my word, I no longer feigned emergencies or climbed over rails. I was allowed to use the bathroom. My nurses were kind, efficient, and often joked with me. I became a "good" patient. The painful penicillin shots left my legs aching, yet I had earned the distinction of "best shot-taker on the floor."

I had come to love these people. I was released and sent home several days later.

Shortly after my return my mother fell ill. It was her estranged father who agreed to pay for her hospitalization which required a rather distant trip to Omaha. She had two miscarriages in short succession shortly before the birth of her fourth child. My father would repeat that she was "sick" in rather vague terms as her nearly one-month-long hospital stay continued. I remember having a rather stern housekeeper who kept us while my father worked. When my mother finally did return she was happier than I had ever seen her; I remember how she danced a jig around the house. I had never seen my mother dance, much less to dance so gaily, and then she disappeared for another set of weeks. I was told she was back in the hospital. All of this was spoken in hushed tones and was most mysterious to me. All I was told later by my mother, in a shamed voice, was that she had been given "shock treatments." I remember my father's repeated instructions that I was to help her at every opportunity and I took those words to heart. I prayed nightly, on my knees, that God would make my parents happy. I attributed the unhappiness to this mysterious illness as much as anything else, and I felt the responsibility to somehow be the one to change the situation.

About a year after my mother's illness I recall my mother's one and only outpatient visit. We all accompanied her to Omaha this time as she had decided to take us to the zoo. It seemed to me that she felt a burden to prove that there wasn't a problem and there had never been one. The determined look on her face said that under no circumstances would she submit herself to any more shame.

As I look back I realize that it was my mother, more than anyone else, who was responsible for my choice of nursing as a life's profession.

Success

My high school years were a time of accomplishment and happy memories. In particular, my band director went out of his way to help me learn the satisfaction of achievement.

At age eleven I begged to play the flute and, reluctantly, my parents rented me a very used instrument. A year behind my peers, my band director helped me "catch up" with the rest of the class. Convinced that I had talent, Mr. Taylor then went to my parents' home. Respectfully he began by saying that he knew they had the best intentions for me. Then he told them that, if they would buy me a quality instrument, I would be an exceptional flute player. I watched the verbal exchange with wonder as Mr. Taylor somehow came away with the promise that they would indeed do so. Over the next six years I never did hear the end of how "we spent three-hundred-fifty dollars on that flute!" but, thrilled with the opportunities it provided, I didn't mind.

Mr. Taylor was my band director from sixth to twelfth grade. When I had smugly achieved "first chair" he encouraged another flutist to "challenge" me as he knew I hadn't been practicing. When I lost the chair, I fought to regain it. Mr. Taylor affectionately called me by my last name and somehow always knew how to motivate me. My ninth grade year he told me I would be entering the district competition as a soloist. I was scared but didn't argue, and he coached me through all the way to a "one" at state level. After I repeated the feat in tenth grade, Mr. Taylor announced to me that I would be entering again in eleventh grade and, once again, he would be choosing my music. He chose an impossible number with thirty-second and sixty-fourth note runs entitled "Le Papillon" (the butterfly). When I complained insistently that it was impossible for me to perform, Mr. Taylor brought a professional flutist from a nearby college to my high school and had him perform it for me. As Mr. Taylor simply didn't hear my protests, there was nothing to do but to get on with doing the impossible. I worked until I felt I could perform some semblance of the number. Practicing after school, Mr. Taylor would often invite others to watch and listen to me. Once I struggled with an impossible run of notes while the most popular cheerleaders looked on at Mr. Taylor's insistence, and all I could think was "who would have ever guessed this?"

I received the coveted "one" at state although, on some level, I never quite felt I deserved it knowing I had missed notes. Mr. Taylor was very pleased and happy for me. Most importantly I had learned the lesson that "impossible" is only a negative mindset.

My parents did not attend any competitions. They occasionally attended a band concert.

I paid for my own baton-twirling lessons at age thirteen and was chosen as a majorette in high school. I taught baton twirling to young girls in my community to earn spending money. I had other jobs during high school, but this one was the most rewarding and the most profitable.

In a graduating class of less than one hundred I had the opportunity to develop my talents and begin to learn what my weaknesses were. I was a member of band, orchestra, choir, and a small performing group. I was awarded a high school music achievement award from a nearby university, the Daughters of the American Revolution good citizen award, and served as president of National Honor Society. I graduated fifth in my class.

There were over eight hundred applicants to my school of nursing. Of these, one hundred were chosen, and we lost half of those the first year. Being selected was an honor I accepted, perhaps, with too much pride. While my test scores were very good and my psychological profile fit, my struggles to overcome my early years would first make themselves known in this endeavor. I often could not relate to people. I first remember this being apparent to me when I met other students with family and financial support for their schooling. I *knew* it was wrong to be jealous but I had to admit to myself that I was jealous. I rationalized that my background made me stronger as I had to do most things entirely on my own. I would later decide that "entirely on my own" was not necessarily a way to develop strength.

Being employed at the hospital after our college classes were completed allowed us to pay for our education without any debt upon graduation. I worked "double shifts" on the weekend and sometimes, one shift during the week.

The diploma program I was enrolled in was federally assisted. We lived in a dorm, if we chose to, that was connected to the hospital by a tunnel. We soon learned to use it. In the middle of a high crime district, one of my classmates unknowingly crossed the street to Kentucky Fried

Chicken the first evening we were all together. She returned and breathlessly told us of the robbery she had been caught up in.

My friend's parents gave me a can of mace. I thought this rather strange as I was not use to having anyone concerned about my safety. I remember having my finger on the "trigger" many times, but I never had to use it.

Two distinct memories of my years at my alma mater remain with me. I witnessed a mother with a sick baby being turned away in the emergency room presumably because the baby "wasn't that sick," although I suspected the fact that she didn't have insurance was the real reason. I also witnessed hub caps being stolen in the parking lot despite the security cameras. I wondered if the thief was related to the mother with the sick infant.

I was assigned a roommate who stayed with me for the entire three years of nursing school. I have often thought how necessary she was to my graduation. Kelly was with me through the ups and downs. We had similar rural backgrounds and could relate in many ways. Her mother had attended college, and she had expectations for her daughter that became my expectations.

Psychiatric nursing was an eye opener for me. My instructors took me aside to tell me I had a gift in this area. I couldn't help but think that my "gift" was no more than being nice to one's relatives. I had the distinct privilege of meeting Dr. Karl Menninger who was then in his later years working at the Kansas Reception and Diagnostic Center (part of the Kansas prison system) in Topeka, Kansas.[2] I was one of three fortunate nursing students chosen to sit in on an interview that he was conducting with a young rapist. The venerable elderly man asked us, after we sat wide-eyed through the interview, "What do you think?" We looked at each other in helpless compliance to his request and finally replied "he didn't seem very sorry." Our answer seemed to please him.

Our final course was called "team leading," and it was a disaster for me. I was so nervous in front of a team of nurses that I would often focus so hard on remembering *every* detail regarding a patient that I would forget *any* detail. I was fearful of angering any member on the team by asking something that she might not want to do. I vowed to stay away from "teams" for a while. Little did I know at the time that I would be assigned to some solitary assignments.

I came to know Joanne my senior year when we were given the privilege of moving to a townhouse that housed four students. The housing was extremely nice and very affordable as it was part of the federally-assisted program. Jean and I shared one bedroom, and Joanne and Kelly shared another. Joanne and I shared similarities in our backgrounds. We were both Catholic, from families with several children, and on our own. I had never met anyone quite like her. She was a spring breeze on a sultry day, a smiling angel telling us we needed Baskin-Robbins ice cream rather than another hour of study, and a vivacious loving presence. I really liked her. I was quite surprised when the gossip mill produced the rumor that she had tried to commit suicide twice by taking overdoses. How could this be? She talked to everyone.

And then she talked to no one. It happened rather suddenly. One day she offered me the poetry that she had written over several years while confining herself to her room. Perhaps all she wanted was a critique, but sirens were screaming in my head as I called the suicide prevention line. It is no joke that they put me on hold. Eventually I was given an appointment for my friend at the free mental health clinic. As I handed her the appointment time I expressed my concern. Her face fell and she somberly met my eyes. "Rose, they don't help you in those places."

As suddenly as she had become morose, she later regained her vivaciousness, although with a new twist. She began to meet every man at the door with behavior bordering on seduction. My roommates were outraged when their boyfriends were accosted. Perhaps I was more generous; however, when asked if I was in agreement that she should be asked to move out, I don't remember voicing an objection.

Within weeks of this development we graduated. With fitted white uniforms starched and pressed and a stage decked with honor and the honorable, we proceeded one by one to gain our admission to the professional world. It was a proud moment.

I married the first boy I had dated within a couple of weeks of graduation. I had asked Joanne to attend the guest book at my wedding but she declined. On my wedding day, a few minutes before walking down the aisle, Joanne suddenly appeared, all smiles, and announced that she had changed her mind. I helplessly told her that I had asked someone else. I'm not sure that she stayed for the wedding.

One month later my class was all together again to take our nursing boards (exam) in the capitol city. The heat was in the nineties, and the all-day exam had been grueling. Gathered after the test in a common room, there were perhaps one hundred of us together when a sudden commotion caught our eye. Having a grand mal seizure in the middle of the floor was Joanne, with only one friend attending to her. I remember a group of nurses being shocked. *How ironic and how very cold*, I thought, that a group of nurses could not have been more compassionate.

My younger sister enrolled in the nursing class two years behind me. She brought me word in the fall that Joanne had been admitted with a brain tumor, and she was going to have surgery to remove it. I remember suddenly being hit with our cruelty in asking her to move out. I was busy with my first nursing job in my hometown, working night shift and sometimes assisting with deliveries and newborn care. Whatever my excuse, I did not go to see her. Eventually the tumor was removed and it was found to be benign. This miracle behind her, one might have thought it explained all of her behaviors and the problem had been dealt with. But shortly afterward my sister brought me another bit of news: Joanne had taken an overdose and died.

Security

The words spoken to me frequently as a child, whether or not in jest, I took to heart: "Well, you aren't too ugly; maybe someone will marry you."

I married at age twenty. Mike and I had dated since I was fourteen. I don't know that I considered that a husband should meet any of my needs; I believed that it was enough that he wanted to marry me. I had an extremely low self-esteem hidden by a sweetly transfixed smile. Mike was a year older than me, in his last year of college, and an army ROTC student. I was terrified when I discovered, after we married, that he would be an officer. This reveals how well we communicated. What we had in common was dysfunction. His family was alcoholic, socially active, and humor oriented. My family was depressed, somewhat isolated, and religious without the joy that accompanies the real thing. I often would think that my husband spent his formative years in a carnival while I spent those years in a funeral home. Ours was a case of opposites attracting.

I was determined to make it work.

I worked while Mike finished a four year degree that took him five years. We had been married less than six months when, for the first time, he simply didn't come home one evening because he had decided to go out with a female classmate and celebrate her birthday. I understood. I bought him the new car that he wanted. I moved when the army decided it was time to move. I worked evening shift on a medical/surgical floor, sometimes working double shifts to buy a washer and dryer and other essentials when I joyfully learned that we would be having a baby. After being commissioned Mike confined his drinking to social events on the weekend, for the most part. Our first child, a daughter, was the joy of my life. As I held her I remember thinking that I had never loved anyone so much. Our son was born two years later, and I cried for joy that I had been given the son I asked for. I had been fearful of praying for a son; my relationship with God did not allow me to ask for too much at this time. We moved, and then we moved again. I had little time to develop a support system. My children were three years and fifteen months of age when my world began to spin out of control. I first had trouble falling asleep and would often wake up from a nightmare that seemed so real as to be a warning. My daily routine was such heavy drudgery as to be nearly impossible to complete. My legs felt heavy when I went for my morning run. Even the morning cup of coffee tasted bitter. A wall of darkness had suddenly enveloped me, and I felt helpless to move past it.

Summoning all my courage and resources, I sought the services of a mental health clinic. I was first asked to write my life's story so as to give an indication of my background. I was then given a dexamethasone suppression test which gives an indication if there is a chemical component to the depression. It was positive. I was scheduled for counseling. It was perhaps my second visit when, as I walked out of the clinic door, I suddenly was terrified to get in my car. Retreating to the security of the clinic I implored for a solution from the clinic secretary. Quietly and professionally she took me back to my doctor's office, and he suggested I be admitted as an inpatient. I was as surprised at this suggestion as I was at the conversation he then had with my husband on the phone. "I think your wife is having thoughts of harming herself." I did not believe this was true. In my mind it was an unknown "something else" that I was terrified of. I agreed to be admitted.

I was escorted to a very nice, secure unit that, in my mind, would have been a pleasant place to work. I put on my nurse persona because I certainly did not see myself as a patient. I had a nutritious meal in a quiet cafeteria. I was one of several nicely-dressed patients. We did not particularly look deranged. Yet I caught a glimpse of a small room with padded walls and doors, and my heart began to race. I was suddenly seized by the "something else" that shrouded me in unidentifiable fear. I had a conversation with a seasoned, concerned nurse who was promptly on the phone making a call. She then asked me to come with her, and my trust in her professionalism urged me to comply. Suddenly I was behind locked doors in a confined area. Nurses were coming at me with medicine in little cups, apparently unaware that I *was* a nurse. We obviously did not agree as to what I needed. I refused. Panicking more and more as the offers were made, I refused to digress from fearing this "something else" to needing inpatient psychiatric care and medication. How could I possibly need this locked room? As one after another nurse firmly insisted I needed the medication, a technique I recognized, I was a caged, wild animal trying to preserve my life. I moved from the small common area to an adjacent patient room. A golden sunbeam cast light directly on me as I flung myself onto the bed, and the thought raced through my mind that God was with me.

Six or seven kind but firm hands knew just where to apply the pressure as I was pinned down still screaming. No matter how I struggled I had most certainly lost the battle that doomed me to my mother's fate. An injection needle found my backside. I cried softly as I drifted off to a drugged sleep.

Kind hands softly removed my running shoes.

A Drug-Enforced Haven

I awakened to an anguish I had never felt before. I could not determine the cause any more than I could end the extreme discomfort. My vision was blurred, my mouth was dry, and my thoughts were prayers. I wanted to run, but there was nothing to run from, nor any place to run to. I was trapped. A voice was singing the "Our Father" from a nearby room. The voice belonged to Nathan, the other patient in ICU.

I was given breakfast, served opposite the other patient who was near my age. He announced that he was bipolar. His appearance frightened me. The wild tremor in his voice matched the constant tremor of his hands which, he said, was due to lithium. His wife was home with his baby, and she needed to go back to work because his illness kept him from working. I could not eat. I could not sit still. I was later to learn that I had akathesia, a side effect from the antipsychotic medication I was given. I compliantly took the next dose. I compliantly did everything.

I was allowed out of the ICU with an escort. I passed zombies, in my opinion, who were walking, drugged and compliant, like myself. I wondered if we were all deranged. I was told that I could attend a morning devotional if I chose to. I thought *of course!*

There would be an answer to this madness that would make itself known.

I shuffled into the common room with my escort just as my psychiatrist started to read from *Huckleberry Finn*. I recognized the words from the book I had read as a child. How could one use Mark Twain's writings in a devotional? Wasn't that breaking every religious rule I had learned? I listened, looking for answers. The prayer followed, and perhaps, the magic would be in the prayer. I desperately wanted magic. I wanted a definite answer and an instant healing. Instead, I was being asked to face the reality that I was dealing with mental illness and all that that would entail. As I was escorted back to ICU we passed the "quiet room" with its padded protection and the only words that came to mind were *why me?* My mind immediately answered this question with something I had recently heard on Robert Schuller's *The Hour of Power*: *why not me?*

Soon a third patient arrived in ICU. Also in her twenties, she had a plastered smile on a face with glazed eyes, supported by a neck that only turned with her body. Her appearance scared me. I forced myself to engage in conversation. She had decided to take her two children and leave her abusive husband when a car accident injured one of her children and caused her to become hysterical. Her husband now had control of the children.

I was assigned an inpatient counselor. A female psychologist patiently sat opposite me for at least three forty-five minute sessions while I had nothing to say. When I finally did speak I could only plead that I needed to be home with my children who needed me. No amount of reasoning would change my mind. I was nothing if not strong-willed. Finally, in desperation, a compassionate doctor let me return home for a day. The stark realization that the agony would follow me to my home hit me fully. I had to get well to return home.

Many sessions after we had begun, my psychologist asked only one question: "Will you tell me about your mother?" I had already told her that my childhood was "fine," brushing the subject off very quickly with a single, apparently non-convincing word. There was my usual long silence, but this time a deep sob came from someone else in the room. I will swear that it wasn't from me.

My hospitalization lasted sixty days, all that my husband's army insurance would allow. I reluctantly agreed to outpatient therapy after I was released. As my mood had shifted and the drugs had been discontinued, the doctors had cautiously but hopefully advised me that perhaps, this was an isolated incident. However, they had not completely ruled out another diagnosis.

I returned home and busied myself with my children and a new hobby, sewing. I had never had time for a hobby before, but it was decided that I should not work for a while.

Within a couple of months I was back in the social circle that my husband's job required. I had never quite been comfortable as an officer's wife. Although I met women I dearly loved, I found myself ill prepared to deal with adversaries. Attending a small luncheon of women assigned to our battalion, the subject of children came up. Another wife who also had two small children, the youngest the age of my son, complained how difficult things had been for her since the last birth. "I certainly would like to have been admitted to a hospital with tennis courts and a swimming pool while someone else took care of my children." Recognizing the description of my psychiatric hospital, I was quite certain the remark was directed at me. For a brief second I considered defending myself as one who had never enjoyed either amenity. But the battalion commander's wife kicked me under the table in recognition of the insult and as my cue to "buck up." How I appreciated that kick.

I said nothing.

A Mountain to Climb

Mike wasn't too sure about all the therapy I was told that I needed, although our insurance paid eighty percent of the costs. I had one group session and one individual session per week. In addition to these Mike was asked to attend a joint session with me. Every session with Mike was the same. Mike would walk in ahead of me, and the social worker would address him by rank and extend a handshake. I would meekly follow and not dare to extend my hand, nor meet the counselor's gaze. With wisdom, concern, and humor the social worker would direct the conversation mostly between Mike and himself. I was barely in the room.

There was something about this weekly ritual, I sensed, that the social worker wanted me to see.

My individual sessions were with the same psychologist I had as an inpatient. She slowly helped me to see the skewed perception of women that I had learned. In my own mind they were inferior to men. My first resolve was not to let this warp the relationship with my daughter or limit her in any way. I realized that I needed to move outside my comfort zone to change this discriminatory view.

My group sessions helped me to see my tendency to rescue. The role I found myself in most often was that of an enabler or a rescuer. In order to do this I had to have a relationship with a victim.

These were painful realizations. Therapy was not fun.

The most profound understanding I became aware of occurred in my group session. It involved a registered nurse in her late fifties married to a minister. She had been one of my inpatient nurses when we first met and had a conversation about a painting. A picture of a boy in a small boat in the middle of a vast lake, the painting had troubled me from the first time I saw it. I remarked that it caused me much anxiety. Her kind response, through twinkling eyes, was that she found the picture to be one of serenity. She then added as an afterthought, "to fear water is often to fear what lies in the subconscious, below the surface." My anxiety had surged with the very words she spoke. Later, when she served as my outpatient therapist, I was often amazed and uncomfortable with her ability to seemingly read my thoughts and intents. One day she missed a session and the other group counselor sadly told us that her minister husband had died. I fully expected her to drop out from that point on. A week later, she was not only present but smiling through tears. Her ability to cope in the event of her husband's death affected me more profoundly than any other influence. I knew she clung to a Rock that I had not yet learned to cling to.

I began to change, although this was not always appreciated. I also continued to require hospitalizations. Two years after my first "episode" my husband was attending an army school in another state for a couple of weeks. Meanwhile I was taking classes toward a hoped for bachelor's degree while I cared for small children. He phoned to tell me that there was nothing to do between classes and wanted to know how much was available on the Visa account. I suggested he read the Bible. I knew his tendency to "party" and that there were also women taking the same course. Whether or not this played on my mind I do not know. It had been several days since I had slept when he returned. He was tired and unaware that I was feeling so euphoric when I crossed the street and announced to our neighbors that I was the Virgin Mary. My husband did not know what to do, but he was advised by a friend to admit me for the second time to the psychiatric hospital.

Reluctantly my doctors gave me a diagnosis and the necessary accompanying stigma. I was bipolar.

Failure

Mania is having all problems solved. Life is wonderful and will always be so. People who do not agree with you simply do not understand. It is the ability to touch others in such a way as to solve all of their problems. It is about the power of divinity. I have lived, I have conquered, and I have arisen.

It is also all about delusion.

A joint session with the same social worker who had counseled my husband and me finally had a different pattern. I did all the talking. Apparently they did not agree, and the expressions on their faces were of intense sadness. At one point I raised a clipboard that held a document I was asked to sign and suddenly broke it in half across my knee. My husband broke down and cried. My only emotion was surprise. I didn't know he cared that much.

Taking pale pink capsules was all right with me. I was told that they were lithium. They were pretty. It seemed to me that they were not accomplishing the intended purposed and, soon, another pill was added. This one made me sleep most of three days. When I awoke I no longer felt euphoric.

I had problems.

One of my neighbors appeared at the hospital about a week after I had been admitted to give me quarters for the soft drink machine. He attempted to reason with me. I was not the Virgin Mary. I disagreed, although I no longer *felt* divine.

I wanted the feeling and the power to return.

Whereas my first hospitalization was sixty days, all my armed forces insurance would allow, my second hospitalization was about six weeks in length. I remember the drive home. My submissive nature and my shame had returned. I turned to my husband and asked "do you think I should tell (our neighbors) that I am really *not* the Virgin Mary?" His reply, spoken in a playful tone, was "I think they know." I wondered how he could be so sure.

For a short time I was somewhat stable. There were gifts from my husband; I remember a tennis racquet, a new swimsuit, and a racing bike. I took tennis lessons. He wanted me to participate in a triathlon with him, which I eventually did. He took me golfing which had previously been his sole domain. He spent time and effort making me feel special.

But I knew, deep inside, that I was not special.

I was faithfully taking my medication, determined not to need hospitalization again. I was certain that I could beat the diagnosis. The problem with my approach to wellness at that time was that it was still all about me. I let few people into my world and the number grew fewer as the gossip spread. It was often difficult to face the people we knew.

What became a severe depression started as an anxiety attack that seemed to grip and paralyze me suddenly one morning and refused to let go for nearly a year.

My first thought in the morning was *Lord, help me live through this day; I don't know how I can do it.*

I went through all the motions of living with all the life drained from me. I was desperate for a solution to my crisis. Whereas infrequent Scripture readings and random messages from the clergy had been my pattern since I was a child, I now searched frantically. I understood how people could commit suicide while I firmly believed it was a sin to take a life, including one's own. I had to live for the sake of my family.

I watched *The Hour of Power* and listened to James Kennedy on the radio. Eventually I read every psychology book I could find in the Ft. Carson library. I felt these to be my lifelines, and I knew I was only hanging by a weak thread.

I found many inconsistencies from what I had been taught as a child and what is true. This can probably be said no matter what denomination a person grows up in. The verse that struck me most profoundly was, "The Lord is my shepherd, I shall not want" (Psalm 23:1).

I do not think I was taught that it meant we are not to ask for anything, but certainly that was the conclusion I reached. The actual meaning, that we will not *lack* for anything struck me like a flying a brick. My first thought was that I needed to enlighten my entire family.

I lost track of hospitalizations after the second. There was a third and a fourth during this severe depression. There were also brief times when I seemed well. I tried to give my children the attention they had missed out on. I went back to school. Eventually the army gave us orders to move, and I was cautioned to be very careful about the amount of stress I took on.

My husband had finished his master's degree, while my bachelor's degree was still unfinished when we moved. His career was progressing nicely as I had been in the "exceptional family member" program and his assignments were changed accordingly. One of the wives joked one day that the army had given him an athletic scholarship to finish his degree as she saw him running or biking every hour during his lunch hour.

Our next permanent move, to Oklahoma, was not exactly bleak. We found a nice town and bought our first house. Our children were in school. Eventually I took work in a nursing home and later, a small hospital. I really didn't know how much I had missed my nurse friends until I rediscovered them. We seemed to have similar backgrounds, similar values, and similar thoughts. The staff was most kind and understanding of my illness, which I divulged. I was given a longer than usual reorientation to nursing. I was also given leaves of absence for more episodes of mania followed by depression.

The insurance that covered up to sixty days of inpatient psychiatric care per year would send statements with the amount of the bill my insurance had covered. When the total amount reached half a million dollars I meekly concluded that I felt indebted for that which I never could have paid. I also wanted to give something back when I recovered.

Then the cord that our marriage dangled from began to unravel.

After writing poetry in a manic state I was perplexed, once in the depressed phase, as to its meaning. I was seeing a psychiatrist who was a practicing Catholic working in the same small hospital of my employment. He eventually changed my medication from lithium to a medication for seizure activity. Another antipsychotic was later added. I sheepishly brought something I had written, wanting a second opinion, not knowing if he would give an opinion. The poem began,

> The problem with the human race
> As far as I can see
> Is that Eve had an ugly face
> And beauty marks of three

Without adding or detracting anything my doctor spoke his mind, that this might possibly suggest some kind of sexual abuse. He did not say that I had been abused, and I did not think so.

I simply turned crimson.

I sat frozen for a long moment while thoughts ran through my head. Memories had begun to surface recently and I wasn't sure what they meant. I recalled how I always buttoned the very top button on my blouse as a child and my mother would laugh about the tendency. I remembered how she laughed that I refused to wear anything sleeveless.

I remembered how I hated hugging my father when asked to do so. I actually had to force the required hug. Later, when alone, I would recall the baths. My father frequently gave my sister and me a bath. I could not recall that he was ever willingly involved in any aspect of childcare, which made this all the more strange.

Because I had grown so quiet during therapy sessions, my doctor asked the reason. Eventually I confided the memories. He asked if I would like to see the psychologist who helped to diagnose sexual abuse.

I remember, what was to me, a sordid session while I looked at pictures and was asked their meaning. My facial expression conveyed one meaning; my words tried to go in another direction. My doctor later told me that it was possible that there was something of this nature in my past.

I felt sick at the possibility. My mind refused to consider the obvious. For a while my world was viewed through smut-colored glasses. Meanwhile my husband had turned to pornography. It started insidiously with his viewing of the playboy channel through blurry lines intended to block the viewing. If ever we were near a TV with a clear picture, he would tune in faithfully.

Before we left Ft. Carson Mike had joined exercise classes that his secretary attended. I was too depressed to care. After we moved he became involved in planning a reunion. The planning sessions involved a former classmate. At first I heard all about her. Later I only heard that she had called him at the office and he had told her not to do so. This bit of news seemed to have the tone of a confession. Again, I was too depressed to care.

My mother had long insisted that shock therapy was the answer to my problems. I had refused this suggestion until I reached the point that, in my mind, I believed my family was better off without me. I recognized my dangerous frame of mind and, in desperation, I finally complied. My doctor did not do such treatments. I found another facility that still used shock therapy as a last resort. One of my neighbors tried, frantically, to convince me that shock therapy was the work of the devil. Another neighbor quietly told me that she had added my name to her prayer chain. I believe that I needed to hear both points of view.

I was admitted to an old hospital in another city. What I remember most, after two weeks of three shock sessions per week, is that I did not remember. The clothes in my closet were completely unfamiliar. My children were wide-eyed upon my return when I could not recall how to use a fork during a family meal. However, my dark mood had lifted and, I believe, I had been given a small window of time within which to act.

I was accused, falsely, of not taking my medication. These accusations came from family who were not near enough to know. My husband was not involved enough to know. I had taken my medication faithfully but, my living situation was so completely intolerable that, unless changes occurred, I was convinced that my episodes of mania and depression would not subside.

The word *divorce* had come up in my conversation practically every manic episode. I would gaily tell my husband how much better off he would be since I was the Virgin Mary, intended to save the world or a similar scenario. In looking back I believe there was a healthy, intact mind trying to flee an intolerable situation. I did not openly admit the possibility that he was unfaithful any more than I admitted that I was not stable.

I tried once again to finish my degree and flunked my first college class. I refused to attend the Christmas gathering at his family's home as we had always done, daring to openly accuse them of alcoholism. Mike was furious. When he insisted on taking the children and going without me, I used my time off from work to drive to Colorado.

I had never been anywhere by myself. I put eight hundred dollars worth of merchandise on a credit card during a shopping spree at a mall. Then I was hospitalized. Mike had to come get me.

This would prove to be the final straw. As this was my first spending spree, Mike also intended that it would be my last. The rules in our family had been quite simple. I was allowed to make money. I was allowed to spend money on therapy, provided we had insurance. I could purchase necessities, such as food. Our clothing was homemade or very inexpensive. Mike spent the remainder. He had heard all the stories of bipolar patients spending large sums of money, and he was not about to lose any more money.

He wanted a divorce.

I really didn't care. Depression over the divorce wasn't any worse than depression during the marriage, but my heart ached for my children, and I did not intend to give them up. Mike was holding all the cards as the successful army major who had just been named Army Teacher of the Year. I was his paranoid schizophrenic wife, per exceptional family member program enrollment. I reasoned that the children, who were ages ten and seven, should not have to move or change schools or have their lives disrupted any more than necessary. Mike agreed, although he refused to move out or give me control of anything. I would have to be the one to leave. I thought it might give me time to definitely put it all together without his abuse affecting me.

Mike and I agreed to have a friendly divorce. I rented an apartment at the end of the street, close enough to be within walking distance for the children. We told the children that my illness was forcing the decision, and that it would be for the best. Their young hearts were broken. I desperately wanted to spare them pain, but there wasn't a way to do so. Mike told me he had hired a lawyer who would represent both of us so expense could be spared. Naively, I agreed. He told me I should buy a new car so I would have a safe vehicle under warranty. He told me which car, which color, and which dealership. Again, I thought he was genuinely helping me so I agreed.

Then he divorced me, leaving for me the few possessions I had been able to carry with me and three thousand dollars. He had painted me as a hopelessly ill woman who would never recover, who had already spent everything on therapy, and who recently bought herself a new car. He eventually took the house, the portion of retirement fund that I was entitled to, the 401K savings, and, most difficult to forgive, the children.

It Only Seems Like More Than I Can Endure

My illness was no longer covered by insurance. Insurance coverage was not a subject of concern during the divorce proceedings. My ex-husband told me that I would probably be better off without any, and I wasn't certain but figured that he was right.

I tried to do all the things that I had learned to do through therapy groups. I found a divorce support group through a church. I was working two twelve-hour shifts on the weekend and getting full time pay at work. I bought the furniture I needed. I spent gut-wrenching time with my children who were going on without me. I cannot describe the pain at losing them. I ranted and raged at the God I thought I served; the pain was more than I could bear. If what I wanted most was to be a wife and mother, Satan could not have struck with a mightier blow. I sought the advice of my pastor. Mike and I had been in a marriage support group prior to the divorce. Mike entertained the group and spent most of the sessions laughing. As this was the fourth church we had attended since the latest move, no one in the group really knew either of us. Mike was comfortable with this. I had prayed for another social worker like our first counselor. I seemed to be the villain in this group. I was simply the woman who could not find anything to smile about. The pastor had nothing to offer.

I continued to see my doctor who was then, at least with facial expressions, giving me his opinion of my ex-husband. Prior to the divorce he had contacted him by phone many times in my presence to talk with him of my progress or lack thereof. I couldn't hear the response, but I now imagine what it must have been.

I made at least one trip through my old house, occupied by my former family. I couldn't help but notice that Mike had purchased new clothes, which were nicely laid out. I marveled that he could feel so gay as to consider new clothes. He was actually considering much more.

My children came to me with the news that Mike's secretary, a young woman in her early twenties, was staying at the house with her baby. She was an extremely attractive unwed mother. Mike said he was just "helping her out." I went to the house to speak privately with her that his arrangement was not appropriate for my children to watch. She moved out and Mike confessed it was probably for the best as he found her extremely "tempting."

Mike received orders for Europe during this time and there wasn't anything to hold me in Oklahoma. I made the fateful decision to move to my former hometown where my family of origin lived. I made this decision in haste and desperation, completely unlike the move I would make later in life. Much later I would learn to carefully consider employment options, medical insurance, and doctors available. At this point I simply wanted to flee the pain of a failed marriage, lost children, and pretty young secretaries.

I borrowed my father's truck and moved my belongings with help from Mike on one end and my father and brother on the other end. I rented an apartment in the same complex Mike and I had lived in after our marriage, while he was in school and I was working night shift. I had not been ill then so I thought it a good decision. In fact, I had decided I could *will* myself well. I wanted to believe that my entire problem had been the marriage and when that ended I would be whole. I took my medication, albeit I started to miss doses. Wellness was no longer my first priority; ending the pain was my first priority.

I took a hospital position that I recognized, within a week, was a bad position for me. It was not at my hometown hospital; I was too ashamed to reapply there. It was in a nearby town. Rather than call to notify the staff that the position was unacceptable I simply did not show up for work one night. They promptly fired me, calling my mother to tell her so. My life was in shambles.

I took some cash and got in my car with a change of clothes and drove. I had no particular destination. I was simply fleeing. I didn't have money to spend on a motel so I spent the night in the car. In fact, I spent more than one night in the car. My father and mother were aghast that I had been fired from my job and, probably feared that they would be supporting an adult child with a bipolar diagnosis.

I bought a house in my hometown shortly before this escapade since I still had credit to do so. It was a very old bungalow with a front porch and enough bedrooms for my children to visit. I had not yet moved in.

My memory of events from this time on will not be entirely accurate, although it is still my memory of events. Doctors would later say that I was manic during this spree. All I knew was that the pressure was off, and I was considering what on earth I was supposed to do next. Of all places I might have landed, I ended up at Ft. Leavenworth in Kansas, not my state of residence. I had originally intended to go see friends, the couple who lived across the street at Ft. Carson. Also a major, the man who brought me quarters for soda lived there with his wife and family. His wife was also a good friend. After driving on the army post, I became uncertain where they lived, and my thoughts were not organized enough to call and ask. I drove until I came to a grassy hill across from a cemetery. On a starry summer night, such as I had prayed under when I was a child, I parked my car. I was wearing a family ring that had once belonged to my grandmother. My mother had had the diamond reset and had given it to me with much ceremony. To me it represented three generations of miserable marriages probably related to illness and lack of treatment or understanding. I flung it out the car window into the night. My mother would later find this most unforgivable. I got out of the car, walked down the hill, and looked into the vast expanse of sky. I prayed with the fervency of a child in a setting that had always made me feel close to his almighty glory and vast purposes.

I admitted that I was completely lost and that I had made a hopeless mess of my life. The tears that heretofore had been held back streamed down my face as I sobbed nearly uncontrollably. Was I crying for myself, my children, or my lost family? I do not know. All I know is that when the answer came it was really quite simple. Directions from the Almighty are often simplistic, the advice you would give to a lost child who simply needs to know the next step. This is all the child has the capacity to receive; she could not understand or bear up under any more.

I was told to walk down the hill.

At the bottom of the hill was a hospital. I walked into an

admission area still crying uncontrollably. The hospital and these people, were the only family I had ever known. They would know what to do. I'm not certain how it happened, but within a short time I was in the back of an ambulance on my way to the state hospital in Kansas. I was there a matter of weeks. It was a rather uneventful hospital stay. I was somewhat stabilized and released.

My father came to get me upon my release, and he represented a family that was now furious. I was aimlessly parking my car at military installations and getting admitted to hospitals, leaving him to retrieve the car and come get me. Who would pay the hospital bill? I assumed I would. I was then back in my apartment, still without a job, watching old movies when my mother and brother appeared and stormed in the door. My mother wanted me to know how irate she was and what the rules would now be. She brought my brother along who really did not want to be there. After telling me that I *would* be working and I *would not* own a car she looked to my brother for reinforcement. Trapped by her controlling nature he only had a few words for me. "Rose, I have a gun. Why don't you use it?"

Truthfully very frightened of them, I took the car a second time to get away. I arrived at a hotel in a nearby city. I left to get something to eat when I passed a soldier on the street who slowed me down and motioned to a country-western bar, obviously intending to meet me there. We sat listening to country music and he insisted on buying me beer as he told me of the Gulf War. I did not need beer; I was already high. I took him back to my hotel, having never done such a thing. When he left I simply got in my car, in the middle of the night, and I drove.

I was on the interstate highway when I suddenly realized that I was headed for the town with my children and

I recalled that I would not be allowed to see them as Mike had remarried within months of the divorce and I was not welcome.

I turned the car around.

I was surprised to see headlights coming at me, and I swerved to miss as many as I could. I don't remember the crash.

Suddenly there was a feeling of complete peace and unshakeable calm. I was in a garden, and birds were singing.

Then, just as suddenly, I was back in the car. A police officer appeared at my window and wanted to know which hospital I wanted to be admitted to. I numbly chose the one that was not my alma mater.

Survival

Several hours are lost to me after the accident. I would later see the car I was pulled from and wonder that I was alive, and, more amazingly, that I didn't have as much as a scratch. I remember that I was angry. I was angry that I was alive and angrier still that I was being asked to live through more pain. I had recently taken an emergency room nursing course and, when the ambulance crew put a Styrofoam neck immobilizer in place in order to pull me from the car, I thanked them with "Styrofoam! How cheap can you get?"

    I remember yelling at the overworked ambulance attendants. I remember being told to get out. I vaguely remember a doctor interviewing me. My next clear memory is waking up on a concrete floor with the back of my head throbbing and two men standing over me tugging at the jumpsuit they were unable to remove. One man laughed as I regained consciousness; the other man fled. I stumbled to me feet, noticing the concrete walls and floor of the men's bathroom. How did I get there? I never knew. Somehow I had the presence of mind to check for blood in my ears, a grave prognostic sign.

Standing at the nurses' desk, I told the psychiatrist who had interviewed me what had happened. He wanted to make sure I didn't want to press charges.

How could I do anything when I had lost my identity, my reasons for living, and my ability to flee? I was powerless, being accused of trying to commit suicide by driving the wrong way on an interstate highway. I denied the charge. I denied the illness. The anger carefully kept in check for so many years was now in full bloom perhaps aided by a concussion that was never diagnosed and an assault that was never questioned. I do know that when I got in my car that night I was not consciously making a decision to end my life.

I was no longer seeking and questioning my behaviors and moods and dedicating myself to change. I was now in survival mode, and anyone who did not understand simply hadn't walked the path I had walked.

"Don't offer me medication! Don't drug me at this time when I most need to be alert. Do you know how many sexual predators, murderers, and convicts are roomed in this facility under the heading 'mentally ill'? Are you as aware as I have suddenly become?"

The driver of the car that I hit called me, concerned for my welfare. She had been on her way to see her sick daughter in the hospital. She wanted to make sure I was all right. I numbly asked her if she was all right, and was assured she was. I don't know that I apologized for hitting her car or thanked her for calling with her concerns. She sounded like a very nice woman.

I was dismissed within a few days and back in the house I bought with my children visiting. I don't remember how I arrived at my house or what persuaded Mike or my mother to let my children visit. I was completely unable to function, but perhaps they desperately wanted me to, so they gave it a chance. I called lots of people in the middle of the night who hung up on me. I was quickly becoming a nonfunctional nuisance without insurance who had no appropriate place to go for treatment. I finally called an army friend half way across the world who listened.

I was relying only on God's mercy to me, a sick sinner. I knew I was a sinner. I knew I had thrown myself on the mercy of his goodness many years prior. Saved people cannot be insane, I was constantly reminded by less knowledgeable individuals. The doctors had a name for it, some kind of mania that is easily kindled, but I was aware that an abnormal response to an abnormal string of events was probably normal.

I had been "grounded" after this accident, without anything to drive. One evening I was in my parent's house, and my mother was giving me yet more guidance that I realized was the road to her life. I wanted her guidance even less than I wanted her life. Suddenly I was seized with terror as I viewed her, perhaps for the first time, not as "sick" but simply as the most manipulative woman on the face of the earth. I ran out of the front door to my house, a distance of two miles, to flee her influence.

Parked in front of my house with the keys dangling in the ignition was an old, used car with liquor and a letterman's jacket in the back seat. The car was unlocked. I was suddenly convinced the car was there for two reasons: so that I could flee from my mother and that this teenager might be taught a lesson. I drove the car to a nearby army post and parked in front of the military police station. I slept in the car. In the morning an officer opened my door and asked if the car was mine. I promptly said "no" and told him it was parked in front of my house and I just "borrowed" it to teach an adolescent not to drink and drive.

The policemen treated my kindly. One of them brought me breakfast and cried as he delivered it. A news story of my ex-husband receiving the Army Teacher of the Year award in Washington, DC, accompanied by his new wife was handed to me. I simply put the paper down. I had nothing to say, but apparently they had figured out exactly what had happened. I was doomed to return to my state's hospital or be jailed for car theft. They contacted my home town sheriff, who also cried, and the decision was made that I would return to the hospital.

The sheriff, a former classmate from high school took me to my hometown to get some of my things. I brought along my guitar. I don't remember the admission process. I was assigned a room on the same floor I had been at before. There were bars on the windows and heavy locked doors. The appearance of the unit was daunting. During my first stay I was too much in shock to be frightened; now I was too high.

I wrote poetry to no one in particular, or, perhaps, I mailed it. My one line of communication, developed during childhood, was letter writing. My grandmother and my aunt had both written me letters throughout my life which had been a lifeline. Now, I needed a lifeline.

One of my roommates was an elderly woman who lay on her bed giggling and talking of the mafia while she stared at the ceiling. A very troubled, very pregnant teenager was another roommate. The third roommate started punching me on one occasion, while we were near the middle of the room. She didn't stop until she had backed me into the corner because, she said, I touched her. With my swollen, bleeding lip as evidence, I demanded she be moved. The answer I received from the staff was a simple "well, don't touch her." The teenager prayed out loud nightly, always emphasizing the third verse:

> Now I lay me down to sleep
> I pray the Lord my soul to keep
> *If I should die before I wake*
> I pray the Lord my soul to take.

I don't remember any therapy or any attempts to communicate with me other than the sessions concerning my possible commitment. I had already been committed once before, under my loud protest, while I was married. I did not think my parents would have the same power my ex-husband held. I was wrong.

My parents visited once during this hospitalization, if it could be called such. I marveled that they could casually visit as if there was nothing amiss about these surroundings. Had the subject of commitment been brought up? I wondered if they would have any second thoughts at all or if their motives were simply financially related. Money had always been sacred in my family. To finally escape my mother I had simply become too expensive. I mused over the thought.

I made friends with yet another teenager, a young man of nineteen. He had been homeless since he was fifteen and had finally decided to return from California, where he had been living, to the Midwest to see his mother. She had promptly called the police, and he had been hospitalized, or jailed, as I thought of it. He was just as happy as I was, and I mean this sincerely. Is this mania a defense from unbearable pain?

He was released as an outpatient before I was. This status change to "outpatient" meant that one was now free to roam about, homeless as one chose. If living arrangements were attached to the status change they were likely to be, as I was soon to discover, intolerable. I was wearing an expensive class ring that had replaced my wedding ring and, when the young man was released with a fever of one hundred six degrees with plans to hitch-hike back to California, I gave him the ring. I was later approached by the police who wanted to know if my ring had been stolen, as they found it in a pawn shop. The class year and initials had identified me. I assured the police that it had been a gift, and I wondered if my young friend had been jailed.

I dolefully played my guitar for other patients, as it took my mind off what was happening. In my mind I was the nurse sent to tend the sufferers who were not being attended. I met a Vietnam veteran who had been on the street many years by this time. He had outpatient arrangements in Chicago that he would escape from time to time. He had boarded a bus only to arrive at this facility, in a manic state, and was promptly put back on a bus to Chicago. The staff attendant brought me a button he had purchased at the bus station and was told to give me. It read "Someone loves me."

There were several patients to be avoided. The woman who told us she had murdered three husbands promptly told us, the day she was discharged, that she was on her way home to murder the fourth. I, for one, believed her.

The outpatient arrangement was one large building where men and women were housed. The men often congregated around the entrance to the women's room. There were no locks on the doors. The common bathroom was also without a lock. There was one very negligent attendant for this arrangement. I took one look at the accommodations and decided I needed another arrangement.

I was without money, identification, or a nursing license. My family had control of all my possessions, including my house. My licenses were locked up in my mother's bank box. All I possessed was what had been instilled prior to this dilemma. I had the certainty that I was meant to recover completely and that I was meant to thrive and prosper and eventually recover my children and my career.

My ex-husband and his new wife actually brought my children to see me at this time, driving a new Oldsmobile. They announced that they had orders for Europe the following year. Since I no longer had a safe living arrangement, I think we visited in a nearby mall. I marveled at this "kindness."

I bought the clothes I needed for two dollars per sack at a nearby thrift shop run by recovering alcoholics. I played them a song on my guitar, and they waived the two dollars. I stayed with another "outpatient" in another housing arrangement, a hotel that smelled of garbage in the middle of the city. Meals were provided at the hospital and I walked the trek daily, passing drugged and inebriated street people, some of whom I recognized from the hospital, and I bled inside as I walked quickly by, vowing not to become one of them.

After a few months the weather became colder, and winter was upon me. I took employment as a sales clerk, although I don't remember how I got around the identification issue. I remember telling them I was a nurse at the psychiatric hospital, and I didn't consider this a lie. The issue was not questioned for a couple of months and, by then, I had enough money to travel half way to a warm destination on the coast.

I decided to hitch-hike the rest of the way. This was not a logical decision. I have since learned that some head injury patients do not think logically for several months after the injury.

Had I not been in excellent physical condition, I never would have survived the next fourteen months.

Grace

After two months I was asked to wear something other than the used jeans I had come to work in daily, another employee offering me some of her clothes. When I would not produce an address for delivery of the clothes, my employer became suspicious. I was no longer employed.

I spent a large portion of my check on a haircut and perm, something I was used to having. The remainder went for a bus ticket that left me far short of my intended destination.

I will always remember the feeling of getting off a greyhound bus late at night with no money, no identification, no plans for lodging, and my only belongings, a change of clothes, in a used bowling bag. I had never exercised such faith that God would take care of me, but I was certain that he would. My destination was not completely aimless; I had a friend on the coast that had listened to me on the phone. I had never been one to memorize Scripture, but I had learned enough to know that if God was for me no one could be against me. The actual verse, as I learned a few years later is that "if God *is* for us, who *is* against us?" (Romans 8:31b).

This implies you have at least one earthly friend in order to succeed. I was in search of this one friend.

Stepping into the darkness one stop past a small town, I walked along the road in search of lodging for the night. A freight train whistled alongside the road, and the thought entered my mind that I did not have the least desire to throw myself in front of the train. I considered that perhaps depression lifts when action takes over, albeit crazy action by most standards. No sooner had I pondered these thoughts than a police car slowed down to ask me where I was going. I explained my situation; I didn't have anywhere to go. I was given a ride to a very nice homeless shelter where I had my own room for the night. I have since thought that every town should be able to offer such. I ate a meal and showered and slept like a baby.

On at least one level I believed my entire journey would be so easy. I went to a Red Cross office to ask if they could help me in any way. I received a change of clothes. Transportation was not available.

The thought of hitch-hiking did not scare me as it should have. I'm not certain how to explain this. I did not think of myself as an attractive female who might be a target. Probably not yet recovered from a concussion, I was not making logical decisions. I had talked to several hitch-hikers at the psychiatric hospital who assured me it was safe if . . . I can no longer remember what the requirements were to make it safe. Probably because I had listened to the conversation and was following the guidelines, which may have included truckers on interstate highways, I decided it was guidance from above. All of these tip-givers were male. But, as I walked toward the interstate and passed the sign that read "no hitch-hiking" I suddenly became fearful. I was breaking the law. I was not on the shoulder of the highway with my thumb in the air more than three minutes before a truck slowed down to take me in.

There are many details of my hitch-hiking experience that I do not remember. I recall a nice young man from West Virginia who shared conversation and bought me a meal. There was another trucker after him. My luck ran out somewhere between Ogden and Salt Lake City.

I sensed evil the minute I stepped into the truck. The older man told me, among other things, that he had once rescued someone like me. She was a drug addict. He had taken her to a hotel and chained her to a bed and, eventually, returned her to her parents drug-free. My knees were shaking as I contemplated my escape route. This evil man wanted me to know that, whatever he did, he would be doing me a favor. I would like to say I got away with my life and my self-respect. As it was, I only got away with my life.

In the middle of a truck stop, somewhere, I don't know where, he made an announcement over his radio that there was a woman wanting to go to the coast. This time two young men, approximately my age, came to the truck to get me. I went with them, anxious to leave. But my knees didn't stop shaking as I was in their presence. They told me, among other things, that they had learned their business in a few weeks and made lots of money. They had an album of "baby dolls" and wanted to include me. We stopped and I convinced them to let me go into a convenience store with them where I promptly shop-lifted anything that I thought would impress them. They were impressed as only thieves would be. I suspected they were hauling something illegally.

In Reno the truck broke down. I knew it was an answer to desperate prayer. The pair was terrified and decided it had to be hauled in for repairs. In the middle of the garage I simply walked away as they did not dare stop me with so many others watching. I went to the police although not directly. I was given a ride across town by someone caring who worked in the garage. As I had no other plans, I told him to take me to the next truck stop. Once he let me out I was suddenly terrified to get in another truck; reality had set in. I walked into the diner and found a back room that was decorated for the holiday season. It was a quiet area that was empty, and I thought I could gather my thoughts. A decorated tree led me to wander in my thoughts, ever so briefly and painfully, to the Christmas trees I had enjoyed with my children. Within a few minutes I was spotted and identified as a homeless intruder and the security guard approached me gruffly. I don't remember the conversation. I only remember that he drug me, still kicking and screaming, out of the door in exasperation. In my mind I deserved a moment's peace in a quiet environment after what I'd been through. In his mind, I was vermin.

Most of what happened to me in Nevada is lost to me. Doctors would later call this mania from which I was not expected to recover. I believe that the human mind can only absorb so much pain and God, in His mercy, allows anesthetic that sometimes takes the form of mania. This is the best explanation I can provide. Eventually I was taken to another psychiatric hospital and interviewed by those who, at least in my mind, were the police. I told them I had been raped and that there was a truck across town probably hauling drugs. They asked me my definition of rape and, when I replied "not having a choice," they were unimpressed. The interview was concluded. I realized in that moment, sick as I was, that I had lost my rights as a free American. I was now a member of the worthless underclass that was to be tolerated, pitied, and occasionally handed a sandwich. But in the eyes of most people, I deserved whatever befell me.

I remember being pulled out of bed by my hair by a very irate woman who was also very strong. I hit her in the jaw. Having never done such a thing, I was surprised at what I was capable of. I remember that I did not use my real name, yet my real name was discovered. It was decided to send me back to the Midwest I had come from with my parents paying the greyhound fare. They sent ten dollars for food. The last words I remember my doctor speaking to me, after he produced one warm sweater for the journey, were "you can always get off half way."

An attendant who was exasperated with the duty took me to the greyhound station and put me on a full bus during the holiday season. The man sitting next to me offered liquor he was drinking from a sack. Although the successful world may have concluded that I was plagued with illegal drug and alcohol use, the truth is I did not use either. When I refused his offering as well as his advances, he promptly punched me in the nose and got off the bus.

As the ten dollars wasn't enough for more than a couple of meals on my journey home, I decided to put the money in a slot machine when the bus stopped in Las Vegas. I was not one to gamble with money, but I was sure this one time God would provide. Instead, I learned never to gamble.

At the next stop I was met by another Vietnam veteran. As he watched the bus empty he saw me exit, weary and bloodied from my own battles, and he met me with a simple "Oh my God!" I had not envisioned my appearance but can only imagine what it must have been. He shared food, warm clothing, and what I needed most at that point, compassion.

In Salt Lake City I lost my bus ticket for the remainder of the trip. It was now February and snowing. I walked around the greyhound station until I was warned that I could be accused of loitering. I was exhausted, looking for any place

I could lie down for a short while. In desperation I left the bus station and stole a hotel room, which means I found a room that had been vacated in need of cleaning and slept there until I was discovered. When the hotel security told me they would not press charges, I told them I had done them a favor. I remember telling them "your hotel is not secure."

I wondered if God uses street people in His plans. Surely He doesn't use them if they break the law. But, I have asked myself, do not successful people break the law every day just as flagrantly?

Back in the bus station, still complaining to anyone who would listen that my ticket had been stolen, I was finally arrested. This time I was jailed for three weeks. I have often thought that I would not have survived my ordeal without this kindness. I was given my own cell where no one could hurt me, and I ate double portions of food and slept double portions of sleep. I would discover, about this time that I was a full twenty pounds thinner since my car accident, and I was already slender at that time. My physical gauntness scared even me, one who had taken pride in appearance.

After three weeks I was given the option of staying or leaving. I chose to leave and, once again, I walked into the night with no identity and no destination. I walked to a convenience store where a kind person gave me bus fare. The bus driver told me of a shelter. Had the shelter not been run by Catholics I might have fared better. For some reason I felt compelled to tell everyone how angry I was about events in my past. They did not deserve this. They put me back on the street within a couple of days and I was back in a psychiatric hospital within a very short time. Eventually I was once again very exhausted. I had no other choice.

I called my father. I don't know that my mother would

have given me more bus fare and, I think, my father may have had his own agenda, but he sent the ticket.

My mother had already mailed all of my nursing uniforms to Salt Lake City, where I had no residence. I marveled that my family thought I could work at a very stressful job at this point.

I arrived at their home and was greeted with paperwork taking away any remaining rights I had as a mother to my children as I was unfit. I slept for several days.

My father made several comments about me "sleeping all the time." There was never any talk of the events that had occurred in the previous year. My parents were adamant that I would have another nursing job. Within a couple of weeks, after food, sleep, and medication, I went to work at a nearby hospital. Looking back, I don't know quite how I did it, and, more incredibly, I was "floating" all over the hospital. Whenever the assignment was completely unfamiliar and most terrifying, I would remind myself that it was no worse than walking into the night with nowhere to go.

I would have to admit that my faith in God was strengthened when he took care of me on the street. My goal while in my parents' home was to make enough money to move far away. They would eventually make me a ward of the state, completely taking away my rights. This only strengthened my resolve.

More Grace

I moved into my home that had been occupied by renters for the last year. My father helped me move. My children were allowed to visit until the day my mother decided my discipline was too harsh and I was obviously "sick again." My father had volunteered to take my children swimming and, I was told later, they would not be coming back to my house. I had a puppy until the day my mother decided I had left him outside too long. She gave him away to someone who would "take better care of him." My mother would knock on my door and tell me there were too many lights on in my house at night. All of this control was exercised in the name of "love." Meanwhile I was a thirty-five year old registered nurse working a combination of step down ICU, rehabilitation, outpatient care, OB/GYN, and the psychiatric floor.

My children were moving to Europe in the fall, and I decided to wait until then to move. My bills from psychiatric care and hospitalizations amounted to one year of my salary at that point. I was making monthly payments since I could afford them and I had every intention of paying them.

My mood was somewhat stable except for the growing anger that I did not know how to resolve. I recognized my parents as the truly sick ones who had to control an adult child. I finally saw with clarity the interpersonal relationships in my family of origin, and they were stifling and sickening.

I told myself I was no longer suffering from post traumatic stress until the day I could no longer deny it. I was taking an elevator at work, all alone until the doors had nearly closed. At the last minute two strong, tall, young men got on and, before we arrived on my floor I nearly passed out.

There was one final hospitalization near the end of the summer. All of my family members testified at the commitment trial. My mother appeared concerned and tender, every bit the perfect mother. My brother testified that what I wanted most was a car so that I could return to work. My father testified with his head down in a penitent pose that I recognized from his attendance at church. He said that I had accused him of molesting me.

The words stung like fire. I dropped my head to avoid any more exposure to the flames. At the very least this was a lie, and he was guilty of perjury for which I was most embarrassed. At the very most, it was true.

The sentence pronounced, I would now be receiving thirty days of very heavy anti psychotic medication in a state hospital, all against my will.

I called my employer who gave me a leave of absence.

I briefly faced my family two more times. The first was in the hallway after the involuntary commitment. I stood stoic as a statue of marble that could no longer be defaced by their lies. The second was at a trial where my parents asked to be made my guardians, but I was given the option of choosing another guardian. I made a brief speech about having rights in this United States of America, my patriotism suddenly surging. I chose a retired insurance salesman I had never met. My parents were upset that I would no longer be a pawn in their game.

Thirty days later, after daily injections that left me far beyond the word *uncomfortable*, I was given a ride to my house by a former marine who was on disability for a brain injury. He had accompanied a brave pastor who made weekly visits to the state hospital. He laughed that his trade was as an electrician and he was having trouble finding anyone who wanted their house wired by an electrician with brain damage. I had never met anyone so content with so little. He handed me a jug of cold water as he rolled down the windows on his very used car. He then winked and said "air conditioning" as the temperature was near one hundred on an August day. After buying groceries and turning on the water, he left payment at the utilities office.

I drank iced coffee as I thought it would clear my system of excess drug. I had to return to work in a very few days, and I needed a paycheck.

Somehow, I worked. I applied for a California nursing license. I applied for a fresh visa card.

I went to see my guardian to explain that I had acquired a nursing license in California and I was planning to move as my salary would be greater. His response was positive. He agreed that he would move under such conditions.

I had plans to drive, although my father had signed on the car note on a vehicle acquired since my hitch-hiking escapade. I hired movers to move my furniture. I was careful that my family not know of my plans and that they not see me packing boxes On the day I was to leave, just as the movers were finishing loading up the truck, my father and sister appeared. They were fuming mad, screaming to the movers to "put all of that back in the house!" A confrontation ensued and everything I had in the car was thrown out as they drove away with my car, probably thinking they had solved the problem. I sat on the ground, shaking at the thought of being trapped in the same town with them, and quickly called my friend, the sheriff. His kind words to me were simply "that car is not worth fighting over." I then composed my thoughts and quickly packed one gym bag. I humbly asked the movers for a ride to the greyhound station, located in the same city of their destination, and they were so kind as to comply. On the way out of town I dropped off my house keys in my realtor's mailbox, as he had located renters for me.

I bought a ticket for California. As I sat on the bus and it pulled into the darkness, I recalled a vivid dream I had when I first started therapy, about six years prior. I was in my hometown, running away from a family reunion. I was running uphill when I passed a car going the opposite direction, the new car my parents owned when I was a child. I saw the car slow down and finally stop at a graveyard. I had to look behind me to see clearly and, when I did, a vicious, terrifying demon got out of the car and ran after me. I summoned all my strength, turned my head forward, and decided to outrun it.

On My Own

The bus let me off at a downtown station in California late at night. This time I had identification, cash, and a credit card.

I was battling post traumatic stress. I doubt everyone would agree with this diagnosis, but survival on the street and in state institutions is just that. I was constantly on alert as I was constantly on the run. My hyper-vigilant state would continue for a year.

I walked to a sleazy, but nearby hotel and entered the lobby just as a desperate-looking woman with a man on each arm sadly informed me that the bar had just closed. I surmised that she was a prostitute and was telling me my opportunity for quick cash had just passed. I was in another cheap, downtown hotel, and I did not want to call this woman a sister as close as she probably was, but her genuine compassion for my circumstances was the only greeting that I received. I realized she was my sister.

I paid for a room that had a door lock but the bolt on the door was not secure, so I demanded another room. There was a Gideon's bible in the drawer by the bed. I flipped through it, unable to focus on any one passage for very long. There was also a telephone book that I searched through to find my friend's address.

I had called his house and his office since the car accident. The letters I sent, sometimes daily, were written in the language of the mentally ill. They were grandiose, a flight of ideas, or poetry. I sent tapes of my guitar or piano music, accompanied by my voice, often singing to another patient. I also talked to his wife or the office secretary, often insultingly. I loudly demanded attention and I left messages on the answering machine. I didn't consider, until much later, how disrupting and embarrassing this would have been. For me, it was still all about survival. I had decided, at least on some level, he wanted me to survive. In my mind I was being followed by the mafia and they were threatening me and my children. If there was any situation that resembled a threat I picked up the phone and yelled.

I walked from the hotel to a Starbuck's the next morning, read the headlines of a newspaper, bought a mocha, and asked where the nearest used car dealership was. I represented the underclass appearing normal for a few minutes.

I took the bus, and then walked to a dealership where I bought a used car for five hundred dollars. I did not realize that I also had a payment schedule and the car would eventually be repossessed. As I drove away, I noticed the hole in the running board which had been covered by the floor mat.

I drove by the hospital I had contacted for employment. I had scheduled an interview prior to the move and had already taken the required continuing education classes by mail.

I was what is known in psychiatry as a high-functioning bipolar. Had you spent fifteen minutes with me you might have thought I was very outgoing, informed, and capable.

Had you spent an hour with me you would have known differently.

I moved in with a waitress I met at breakfast who needed a roommate.

I was successful in the interview and took a position working as the "swat team" RN who carried a pager and responded to emergencies on a medical floor and in step-down ICU. I started orientation and sat through the first week of required hospital policies. It was the first day of clinical assignment when I realized I could not work. A young woman, about my age, had been admitted from a nearby psychiatric hospital with an attendant since she was a suicide risk. I was assigned to her. My voice became sarcastically louder and louder as I accused my coworkers of ignoring her needs and gossiping about the suicide attempt that brought her to the hospital. I realized my rage, barely controlled, would not allow me to work as I realized, when I attempted to pass medications, that my powers of concentration were nil. I do not remember if I finished the shift; I remember telling someone that I would not be back the next day.

I drove by my friend's house, but had no intention of stopping. When I first met him my husband was in the same unit and he had helped me by developing a running schedule that was tailored to me and, eventually, very successful. I had run several half marathons and had decided, in my early twenties, that I could do anything I truly applied myself to. I had dreamed that I finished a marathon and he handed me my trophy. As I looked at his nice house in a nice neighborhood I realized that I was no longer dressed well enough to go to the door.

The other connection was the name, Daniel. His name, his appearance, and his mannerisms reminded me of the priest who led me to Jesus as a child, and I was in search of guidance.

I attended a worship service with my roommate, who was quickly becoming tired of living with me. The appearance of the church, a non-Catholic denomination, was most strange to me at this time. I was suddenly aware that there was only a rare refuge for the truly desperate. I went forward to be baptized again, the first baptism occurring when I was an infant. I stood after the service, water dripping from the immersion, and asked for lodging. The pastor suggested a lady who needed a roommate, provided that I could pay. I used the money my renters put in my account to pay. I had not paid the mortgage on my house for the last few months and there would be an inevitable foreclosure after a few more months.

I took a job at a nursing home, thinking it might be less stressful than the hospital. I lasted a week.

When I lost the next job the lady who had taken me in asked me to leave. Eventually I found a third woman who needed a roommate and took a job roofing a house. I spoke very briefly to my friend on the phone and I remember three things he told me that, on some level, eventually got through to me: 1) I needed help; 2) he could not come see me; and 3) I was not to call the office. These messages only became clear because he got a restraining order. When I broke the order by showing up on his doorstep, he called the police.

I pleaded guilty to the charge and spent another night in jail. From there I was briefly released, picked up the same evening, and eventually taken to the state hospital. I remember telling someone on admission that I was allergic to every psychotropic medication I could think of, hoping to avoid the severe akathesia that I had once experienced. I then recall a straight jacket that was actually very comfortable because it allowed movement, and a padded isolation cell. There was a brief revelation in my mind that I truly was a danger to myself as I thrashed about until I was exhausted with the activity. There was another commitment. I argued that I did not need help.

A meeting with several health care workers in one room followed. My doctor was present as well as an older registered nurse. I was very surprised to see her holding back tears as we discussed my RN status. I had never seen another nurse cry over me. It gave me hope that there was, indeed, some goodness beneath all the layers of shame. If Rose was truly worth saving perhaps she could one day have her children back.

It would be four years before I would see them again, and seven years before my daughter would come to live with me as a college freshman.

The other impossible dream was to return to nursing. I will not say that the road was easy. I was one of the few, the privileged, to be tied into a good community mental health system that allowed me to eventually achieve both impossible hopes

I was released with a bus token and no particular place to go. I did have a counselor who was following me. As I stood at the bus stop in front of the hospital and looked at the bus token in my hand, it occurred to me that God would use this token to his glory

I returned to the woman I had moved in with before this hospitalization who needed my disability check. If I had not had help filling out the required paperwork for disability benefits I might still be a homeless street person.

During the following summer I lived in a run-down house within walking distance of the ocean. Every morning, after sleeping fitfully and awakening early I would walk down to the marina and drink coffee while I listened to the seagulls. There was something very healing about the ocean air. I would then take the city bus to a nearby restaurant with an all-you-can-eat buffet. Although I had no appetite, I would stay until I had eaten at least a minimal day's nutritional requirements. I was trying to do my part to heal mind and body. I was faithfully taking medication again.

After a few months my roommate demanded more than half of my disability check, insisting I could go back to nursing. I recognized the similarity between my parents and this woman. Perhaps visualizing nurses as women who did little but smile and give injections, they didn't comprehend the stressful nature of the work. But they were aware of the paycheck it could produce. I was given an opportunity to move, and I took it. To her credit, this woman took me to a church down the street that was a mix of army personnel and Korean women. They were very supportive of me. She also took me to a very good chiropractor who successfully treated my subluxated vertebrae, probably resulting from the car accident, that had caused me tremendous neck and back pain.

I moved into an apartment for the disabled with another mentally disabled roommate. I had help filing bankruptcy and handling my money. The only thing that I objected to was not being allowed the necessary money to tithe to my church. I made excuses as to why I needed the sixty-six dollars and tithed anyway.

By the grace of God I avoided the vices of the downtrodden. I lived the life of boredom, lack, and standing in line long enough to hate the poverty that the church of my youth had often idealized. I qualified for a Pell grant and finished an associate degree at a nearby college. I taught the small children in the Sunday school at my church. I volunteered for office work at a nearby hospital.

I both appreciated and hated riding the bus. I stood in

line for the bus, transferred buses, and allowed an hour to arrive anywhere on the bus. I marveled at mothers with several young children in the same situation as I struggled to carry groceries home on the bus.

I stood in line for benefits and check-cashing and the least expensive items on "quarter day" at the nearby thrift store. I walked, and I walked, and I walked.

I came to expect the looks I received when my able body received disability benefits and my able body bought food with food stamps.

I watched as others succumbed to the temptations that could derail me: children being ignored while mom took on yet another boyfriend, theft of food stamps, lies told to received more benefits, drug and alcohol use, and the laziness that might make one want to stay in such a system.

This was my life for five years. During this time I was hospitalized as an inpatient a few times, but only briefly. I continued in frequent outpatient care that included medical management, group therapy, and visits by therapists to my apartment. I also had help with job training and getting back into the work force.

My ability to choose only safe people for my inner circle was improving. I was developing the discernment I had previously lacked.

I also searched and memorized Scripture and delved very deeply into just what was needed for my spiritual growth. The verse that struck me most profoundly was "You do not have because you do not ask" (James 4:2c). I could only remember a handful of times I had dared to ask for anything. To actually be *expected* to ask was more than I could comprehend. I had always expected my children to ask, but to consider myself one such loved child was a step further than I had previously taken my faith. The other verse that

I contemplated was "My people are destroyed for lack of knowledge" (Hosea 4:6). I had to admit that my knowledge of Scripture had been pretty limited and, what I did know had been twisted.

To be mentally disabled means that one can no longer carry on a conversation with the "normal" world. One step below a real human being, the first thing I noticed was the avoidance of eye contact. Even some health care workers would avoid the eye contact that might have made us equals. Without a job, there is no weekend to speak of. Without hope for more than a lackluster existence there is no purpose to speak of. Often there is no family to belong to. I would often stare at anyone trying to make conversation with me at my church and have absolutely nothing to say.

The thought of returning to that "normal" world terrified me. The image that came to mind was one of a boxing prize fighter down for the count. My mind would tell me to stay down on the mat and, although defeat was certain, at least no one would hit me again.

After finishing a job training class I created a resume that seemed to be from a world so distant it appeared to be another life I barely remembered. I needed a miracle.

One afternoon two other disabled young adults were smiling in the apartment courtyard, telling me they had just returned from bowling. Recreation is rare on a meager income. They told me a local businessman took them bowling every week, and they knew he would be happy to have one more join. Bill was a member of their church. After a couple of bowling sessions he offered me a job working in his real estate appraisal office. I knew nothing of appraising or real estate and very little of office work, and I told him so. He insisted, and I agreed, recognizing that an opportunity, even if it not the one you are looking for, is still an opportunity. Little did I know that this would be the man who would coach me back into "real" life and the "normal" world. I was so terrified on my first day of employment as I sat at my desk in his small office of three to five workers that all I did was shake.

He paid me anyway.

A New Definition of Security

Commuting to and from my new job was a burden and a delight. I had lived in a rundown apartment complex in the middle of the city for several years. Every morning I would rummage through my assortment of very used clothing to find something appropriate for an office. I then waited for the bus and transferred twice, a total of a one hour ride, to be let off in a beautiful park in the heart of a small town valley. I was very grateful and bowed my head in a prayer of thanks at the change of scenery. My employment was in a modest building next to a gas station across from the park.

    I would soon discover that nearly everyone in this small community knew and loved Bill. Ten years my senior, he was recovering from his third divorce. His youngest son had been killed in a car accident. His oldest son was in prison. Having made a profession of faith as a child, he told me he turned his life around at age thirty-five. At that time he took his children and moved to Alaska where he studied the Word seriously. He had become involved with the mentally ill when several of them had come to his office looking for a handout. He frequently paid them for washing windows or other small tasks, but did not give free handouts. He also engaged them in conversation, treating them with respect.

At the weekly bowling groups he would minister as best he could to anyone who would listen. He came to know the backgrounds and the burdens of each member of the team. At the conclusion of each session we all formed a circle in front of the bowling alley, which was in a crime-ridden downtown district. We prayed.

Bill's background was simple; his large family had moved from the Midwest when he was a baby. His father died when he was a child. Hard work led him to work his way from the bottom to a management position for a large company. After he retired he took a second job as a real estate appraiser and managed the real estate he bought as rentals. He bought fixer-uppers and did the repairs himself. His wealth gave him the ability to become involved in several community projects and, I was soon to discover, he was most generous.

I was never quite certain what led him to hire me. He had hired several people desperate for a job and, I suppose, he was a good judge of who would eventually succeed in the climb out of poverty. I also think his own experience with excruciating emotional pain led him to help others suffering the same. He knew of my desire to return to nursing and that, at the very least, I possessed an inactive registered nurse license.

When I expressed a desire to live in the same small town to avoid the bus ride, I framed the request more as an impossibility. There were several apartments within a short walk of Bill's office, but I had a checkered background. Bill said that we should pray about it. My own experience with prayer had not included shared prayer. For me, prayer had been quite solitary.

Bill drove me around town and showed me landmarks and locations of businesses that he associated with. As an appraiser's assistant I was soon to learn all the streets and highways in a three-county area. But first I would have to buy a car and relearn how to drive. On one particular afternoon Bill stopped at a very nice brick apartment with a sign reading "for seniors only." It was a quiet street, and there was no more than a passing dream that I could live there. After asking my opinion of the premises he picked up his cell phone and dialed the number on the sign. I was surprised when he did so and alarmed that he might lie as I protested "but I'm not a senior!" He winked as he talked to the woman, someone who knew someone he knew. I heard him say "well, she's not a senior, but she *is* quiet." In a matter of seconds I had an appointment to meet for an interview. I continued to protest "but you didn't *tell* her about the bankruptcy, the misdemeanor, or the mental illness!" In contrast to my negativity Bill was absolutely positive.

I agonized the night before the interview, absolutely dedicated to telling the entire truth. I finally admitted that I needed another miracle. After living for so long surrounded by despair, I had lost the optimism that had characterized my younger years. Whereas I once considered miracles to be common occurrences, I had lived through enough adversity to make me question what I truly deserved. Being surrounded by illness and hopelessness had changed me. Whereas Job had simply worshiped after his tremendous losses with "The Lord gave and the Lord has taken away. Blessed be the name of the Lord" (Job 4:21b), I had come to the conclusion that the Lord had given, and I had never deserved any of it, so the Lord had taken away. Attitudes from some social service agencies, bank tellers, and health care workers reinforced this view. But is it not true that none of us deserves the rich blessings the Lord gives?

We met at the apartment, which had enough room for my children to visit and was within my price range. We had barely exchanged introductions when my future landlord confided that she had prayed about this interview and was absolutely certain she was to rent the apartment to me. In astonishment I then confided that I had prayed for a miracle and returned her confidence with my own circumstances. Every step of my return to the old world with its security of health, job, friends, and family would bring such a depth of gratitude and release from pain that I would sob, sometimes for hours.

A few months after moving into the apartment I had become somewhat proficient at my job. I still became easily flustered and faxed my scratch paper instead of the needed documents to a title company, or I reversed and omitted pages in a thirty-two page document, but by and by, these incidents were becoming fewer. In many ways Bill provided the earthly father's concern and counsel that I had never received. It astonished me when I made, what in my mind, was a tremendous error and he simply smiled and said "it's okay." I sensed healing like a needed balm poured over my wounded spirit in those moments.

Bill had a list of associates from his Kiwanis club that he would consult for everything from used car purchases to home financing for those not easily financed. He bought a round of lattes every morning for everyone in the office and, somehow, that latte on my desk had come to stand for where I was going. Eventually Bill and a lady friend would buy me my first set of dishes, rescue me when my car battery died, take me to their church, and help me move into my first home.

I was no more than somewhat in a comfort zone when Bill walked into the office one day, looked me straight in the eye, and said "I think you should go back to nursing." Bill was, at this point, nothing if not exasperating. It seemed that no matter how hard I pushed myself he would push me harder. I would like to say that I was completely appreciative the day he said this to me, knowing he thought I was ready to tackle my heart's desire, but I have to admit my thoughts were more tuned to "so *now* you get rid of me!" or "no *wonder* three women couldn't live with you!" Still, I had the good sense to keep my mouth shut. And, probably because I was more angry more than I was in agreement, I walked out of the door to the nearest nursing home.

I had eyed this home before. My elderly neighbor had confided there had been some kind of trouble that made the newspapers and the place was in trouble financially because of the bad publicity. Still, it was impossible for me to get employment as a registered nurse. I had not worked in over five years. I had made half-hearted attempts at employment in hospitals, always being told that I could never reenter the work force. As I walked toward the facility, about a mile from Bill's office, I decided that if nothing else, I would prove him wrong. And, if I actually *got the job*, I would listen to him from that point on.

I did not know how I could possibly be honest and gain employment. I prayed. I walked into the facility and was immediately taken to a conference room for an interview with an overworked and desperate director of nurses accompanied by her equally overworked and desperate assistant. I answered questions. Yes, I had a license. No, I had not worked in five years. Yes, I could work any shift. Had I completed a recent "refresher course"? I replied that I had attended a two-week orientation recently at a nearby hospital. What I did not include was that they would not take me on as a volunteer registered nurse. That experience was not exactly a confidence booster. I added, "I'm bipolar, and I have been hospitalized before."

After the interview the nurses told me that, rarely, when the two of them agreed on a prospective employee had they been wrong. They hired me.

I was dumbfounded as I realized I had been hired. Then, I practically arranged my circumstances around this new development. The facility was a two-mile walk from my apartment. I had gone from eight dollars an hour to eighteen dollars an hour in this new job. My first position was administering medication to fifteen patients, full-time, on day shift.

Bill was thrilled for me. I kept the job at the appraisal office part-time because, after I bought a used car, I was planning to buy a house.

God's Helpers

There were many people involved in my recovery. I am reminded of an incident that occurred while I was still unemployed on disability. My roommate was going from church to church looking for help for her bipolar disorder. She wanted free clothes, free food, etc., but did not belong to any particular church. One day the two of us were at a mall when a member of one of the churches offered her a worship service to attend regularly. She replied "no thanks." His reply to her came as a well known parable that my roommate apparently had not heard:

> There was a woman on her housetop because her community had been flooded. She was waiting for a rescue. A man came by with a boat and said "get in; I'll take you to safety." She replied "no thanks; I'm waiting for God to rescue me." Hearing this, he went on. Later in the day a helicopter came by and a rope was lowered. She was told "grab hold; I'll rescue you." She yelled back "no thanks; God will rescue me." Hearing this, the helicopter left in search of others to rescue. The flood waters continued to

rise and the woman drowned. Upon entering the pearly gates she asked the Lord "Why didn't you save me?" The Lord replied "I sent you a boat, and then I sent you a helicopter; what else could you want?"

My roommate was unmoved by the story, apparently preferring the sympathy and the free handouts generated by her tale of woe.

Ella was my supervisor at the nursing home. She was from the Philippines and had come to the U.S. without her family initially, and had worked her way up to the supervisor position while sending money for her husband and children to follow. I admired her as an excellent nurse. I found my work at the nursing home to be a rude awakening after spending so many years working in hospitals. The number of patients each nurse was responsible for was daunting as was the scope of practice. Ella handled it all gracefully and professionally. When I considered the other challenges she had faced, from language to culture to home-buying I stopped feeling sorry for myself.

I met many other nurses from the Philippines. I also met those who had fled from Cambodia, Laos, and Liberia as well as workers from many other countries. Nursing homes are in need of nurses, nurse's aides, cooks, housekeepers, and laundry workers. These jobs are usually not as high paying as hospital jobs, nor do they always have benefits. To some they might be viewed as the bottom rung of the ladder of health care jobs. To others these workers would be considered the angels of our society who guard our precious elderly and infirm. There were many who inspired me to give more and take less. This is the essential secret of happiness in this life.

I would like to say that my bipolar illness vanished overnight as my heart and my hands were busy helping others and I was left with little time to think of my own problems.

This was not the case, no matter how many times I went forward to have hands laid on me at my church, no matter how many scriptures I memorized, and no matter how fervently I prayed I continued to experience highs, although not so high as before, and lows, although not so low. Panic attacks followed by a brief hospital stay would rob me of my first nursing home job about a year after I began.

I had another job the day after I was let go as I was, by that time, a nurse with recent experience and a mortgage to pay. I also had an excellent psychiatrist that I had chosen myself.

Dr. Kim was from South Korea. What he majored in during his many years of education was compassion. The look on his face when I told him, as briefly as I could, of my medical history was genuine. His clothes were often wrinkled because he spent the night sleeping at the hospital. He was dedicated to his patients. I could tell he was also loved at the facility he practiced at, judging by the sign he proudly displayed in his office: "BEST DICTATOR." In small letters beneath this title were the words "medical transcription department."

Dr. Kim was brave enough, when the time came, to allow me to change antipsychotic medications from an old drug that was apparently working to a new drug with less potential for side effects. Many doctors would not have allowed me to "rock the boat."

My second nursing home job lasted six months. During this time the Board of Nursing had decided to put my license on probation for "a mental disorder." I had limits on my scope of practice and was required to have regular reports to the Board from my psychiatrist as well as my employer.

At first this obstacle seemed insurmountable. Bill helped me put it into perspective. When I told him that I was apparently meant to be an appraiser and not a nurse he simply replied "adversity usually means you have chosen the correct path." I considered this bit of information, but I didn't know how I would choose a lawyer for the defense I needed. Bill simply consulted with someone over the phone and handed me a name and a generous check. It was what I most needed, and I was humbly grateful.

On the top floor of the tallest building in the nearby city, I sat in a waiting room for a free consultation. I was greeted warmly by a genuine and knowledgeable lawyer who appreciated my struggle to return to my profession. He was not the first lawyer to be so helpful. The first lawyer, the one who handled my divorce, had also helped me deal with "ward of the state" issues from the previous state. He had charged me only a little. And when I lost everything after the divorce he reminded me that "there is a higher court." This lawyer was also gracious. I confess, at some point, I did tell him my favorite lawyer joke: "why are lawyers buried six feet down? Because, deep down, they are really nice guys." He laughed.

A meeting was arranged with several members of the Nursing Board, and my lawyer, after counseling me, allowed me to do all the talking. I believe my voice may have had a quiver to it, but when the final arrangement allowed me the hope of recovering an unencumbered license, I was most satisfied. My lawyer, to whom I am most grateful, simply told me "you did a good job in there."

My third nursing home job lasted two and a half years. This time I would leave of my own choosing for a facility that provided much better care.

There are other helpers that need to be mentioned. About as often as I changed employers, I also changed churches. While I realize one needs to "stay planted" in order to grow, there is also something to be said for what each church can provide. At one church I took a basic discipleship course. At another I took a course called "The Wounded Heart" which is for those who have experienced sexual abuse. At the next church I took an advanced discipleship course that covered an overview of the Bible. While I had taken Bible study classes since I was in my twenties, I had never taken one with so much depth. I also took a class that explored shame as the basis for addictions. I attended AA meetings with friends. I participated in a program providing food, shelter, discipleship, and hope to the homeless. I would be hard-pressed to mention all the specific people who helped me through participation. The knowledge I gained also helped me at work as I found myself working with others who were troubled.

My fourth nursing home job lasted five and a half years. I would eventually choose to leave to be closer to my children and, later, to return to a hospital environment. While I was no longer hospitalized for illness during those years, I did require more than the two weeks of vacation I was allowed yearly. I had always been honest about revealing my illness to employers. Once or twice a year I required time off without notice. This was not at all convenient for my employer but it was tolerated, and I felt both needed and appreciated. I worked the evening shift as I found it much less stressful than day shift. My doctor had put a stipulation on my employment that I work no more than forty hours per week. I sometimes worked forty-five hours, but I worked fewer than most of the nurses who worked fifty to sixty hours per week. Again, this was not always convenient, but it did seem to keep me healthy. When I did work, I really worked. I usually took one quick fifteen to twenty minute meal break as I found that I worked more effectively with at least one short break.

There were two community groups that helped me

return to the world as I knew it. Bill had suggested that I join a community choir, knowing how much I enjoyed singing. He told me of a choir sponsored by his Kiwanis club and I joined. Eventually we would sing in nursing and retirement homes, which brought things full circle for me. I also joined Kiwanis the year Bill became president of the club. Joining these groups was by no means comfortable for me. I felt as if they could see right through me to the labels I had become: bipolar registered nurse with license on probation who lost her children and filed bankruptcy. Truthfully, I was only known as the alto who sang "God Bless America" before Kiwanis meetings and who worked as a registered nurse in a good nursing home.

My return to society had begun.

A New Definition of Success

Although my return to society was progressing nicely, there were still gaping holes in my personal life. My children were in high school more than a thousand miles away. Mike was on his third marriage, and it was not going well. The first thing his new wife did was to kick my seventeen-year-old daughter out of the house. My daughter was a beautiful girl, a senior in high school, and a straight A student. She sang in the choir, played soccer, and attended church with her brother. I suspected she was a rival.

My daughter was heartbroken. She wanted to finish high school with her peers so she moved in with the family of a friend, and I paid support money. She applied and received a scholastic and a vocal scholarship at a university near me after graduation. As thrilled as I was, I had to seriously consider potential problems with our relationship that my doctor had warned of. For one thing, she was now a teenager and I had not been with her for any extended length of time since she was eleven. The first time she asked for permission to drive the car I nearly went through the roof; how could my eleven year old (in my mind) *drive a car*?

Eventually she would choose to transfer to another college, and I would have to give her up again, although I was pleased she would be near her younger brother who needed her. As a senior in high school he lived in the basement of his father's home or stayed with friends to be away from the unhealthy atmosphere in his home. He was constantly being told by his step-mother that he would end up in prison.

I had made a trip to my ex-husband's home between the second and third wives and was able to see my children in the atmosphere there. To say I was terrified would be an understatement. The bright spot during this fact-finding mission was that I attended church with them and was a little embarrassed when introduced as the long-lost mother. But one elder gave me a jewel I had clung to. He simply reassured me "Momma, you made your mark on them."

My relationship with my son would be mostly long distance. I was able to provide a few words here and there and needed financial support. After he graduated from high school I gave him money to move out into his own apartment. Shortly after that he decided to enlist in the National Guard. One summer, while visiting, I was able to provide money for needed vehicle repairs and new tires. I was overcome with emotion when I received a Mother's Day card thanking me for my support and telling me "I don't know what I would have done if you hadn't been there for me." I was so keenly aware of what both my children had been through that I found it hard to feel I had been a good mother. Still, they survived and thrived.

In due course my daughter married a nice young man who also enlisted as a soldier, and she gave birth to my granddaughter, who was named after me. My daughter brought her as an infant and came to live with me the first time her husband was sent into combat. I cannot verbalize how much healing occurred for me during those months. My son graduated from ROTC, was commissioned as an officer, and married a lovely woman. Two boys were born, one to each of my children, during the next year, shortly before my son was sent into combat. Being with my children and their spouses and holding my grandchildren, I realized how fulfilling life could be. While their childhoods were far from normal, whatever normal might be, they are loving, contributing members of society whom I am most grateful for.

I have been concerned about bipolar illness appearing in the next generations as only one who has suffered from it could be. At age twenty-seven my daughter was diagnosed with a mild form of epilepsy, and she now takes medication. Realizing that there has been a suggested link between some forms of epilepsy and bipolar disorder, I also sought the advice of a neurologist.[3] The suggestion that I could actually have a physical cause related to all the episodes of illness in my life somehow lifted a load from my crippled back. On some level I had internalized the condemnation accrued over the years. Why can I not will the problem away, especially if I am a disciple of Christ as I claim to be?

I am confident as of this writing that, whatever genetics may throw our way, my family will survive. In truth, this daughter of Abraham has been loosed. Perhaps it is easier at age fifty to take five pills a day than it was in my twenties; at fifty we all suffer from something. I have come to accept myself as I am. I see my creativity in my daughter, my boldness in my son, my sweet shyness in my granddaughter, and my ability to overcome in my grandsons. I also see a rather annoying obsessive-compulsive trait that shows up in my work; at times it can be called thoroughness. I have come to understand the perfectionist in me that will never be perfect. I have given myself permission to only be human.

I have come to understand what "perfect" means in the light of Scripture. A perfect Christian is one who is mature in the faith.

Forgiveness is Not Necessarily Reconciliation

I remember the fervent prayer I prayed in my childhood, on my knees, and often with tears in my eyes. I believe that the Lord answers prayers; however, as man has been given free will, the answers are not always as we expect. "Please make my Mommy and Daddy happy" was my constant plea. I thought the problem was related to not enough money, something I was overhearing. I also had other slants on what might be the cause of their misery and I studied the problem constantly, often from my rocking chair.

As a young adult I had an unhealthy need to control. This was born out of fear, for not to control put one at the mercy of another. Painfully, through therapy, I learned that the only person I could control was myself, and I had not been doing a very good job at that. About the same time, I understood Jesus' use of parables in teaching. To see and yet not to see, to hear and yet not to hear was the fate of the Pharisees. The deeper, truer meaning of his words was reserved for the humble, the meek, the lame, and the needy. Only the sinner who beat his breast in humility was to be justified. To be in no need of such grace meant that one could not be justified. I understood, and yet the nurse in me didn't want to let go of "fixing" my family of origin. They were content with religiosity and pretense, and I was the enemy.

Truly, I had come to a crossroad in my life where I had to choose returning to the old Rose, the one they expected me to be, or going on with my life as the new creation I had become. I have often thought this might have been easier had I not been a nurse working with the elderly. My own parents were gaining in years and every brief encounter I had with them, from the time they made me a ward of the state until I fully recovered, was detrimental. I dreaded the visit, had nightmares afterwards, and I missed work as a result. They were never apologetic or concerned about my welfare. My mother would chide me with "and *which* church are you attending *this* week?" My father would come for visits and, as I locked doors behind him, I would have flashbacks from my childhood. Visits with my siblings often left me nauseated. Angry messages were left in my mailbox and on my answering machine as I began to withdraw from them. I had been concerned that *I forgive them* while unaware of the effects of their constant bickering and tension. Oddly, I had never before considered this might be a factor in my illness. While I was someone they cared for and professed to love, I was not someone they truly knew or respected.

It took me a long time to come to the conclusion that *I was no longer willing to let them harm me.*

A dear friend of mine is a retired minister. He was in his eighties when my choir practiced in his home regularly, and soon, I found myself going to him with prayer needs. There finally came a Mother's Day when I didn't send a card to my mother. I agonized over this decision, but it seemed best to completely remove myself from a toxic family. I told John of my decision, as well as my background. His words to me were kind, and somewhat surprising to me. He said, "Well, there doesn't seem to be much you have in common."

I moved across the country not too long after this decision and, for awhile, my address was unknown. Eventually letters and emails from my family of origin caught up with me, and I returned them very briefly and as one might answer a casual acquaintance. These correspondences have lost much of the power they once held, and I am grateful for that. I wish them no harm. I pray for them.

Too little is said about not looking back. What I heard preached over and over is that we should make amends with those who have offended us. But, if the offender is going to continue to offend, if our testimony is not received, my understanding is that we are called to forgive . . . and then "shake the dust off your feet as a testimony against them" (Luke 9:5b).

If there is one commandment that sometimes bothers me it would have to be the fifth. I often think I have never honored my father or my mother. It took me a long time to put this in perspective. Another father, another mother would have been honored by the daughter I was. My parents would only have been "honored" had I pursued a path like theirs, which would not have honored my God. The word *honor* in my concordance, in the original Hebrew, means "to make weighty," whether in a bad sense (burdensome, severe, dull) or a good sense (numerous, rich, honorable).[4] A child should "make weighty" his or her parents without regard to the righteousness of the parent "that your days may be prolonged in the land which the Lord your God gives you" (Exodus 20:12).

The only emotion I felt at letting them go was tremendous relief that I would no longer have to bear the burden and shame that prevented me from achieving all that I was meant to achieve, my true purpose for which I was born.

A New Direction

Leaving the security of my home of thirteen years for a southern destination across the country required much prayer. I consulted my friend John, who prayed me through each step. I was aware that returning to a hospital environment would allow me the benefits that I had lived without for so long. Eventually, I wanted to have enough for retirement.

My children and grandchildren would be within driving distance if I moved. I had considered moving nearer to them, but my decision to provide for myself and take the burden of my future off them was more pressing. I had always wanted to see the east coast. I would be a short distance from both the mountains and the sea, and that suited me.

Bill came to my house one fateful day to tell me that the real estate market in my valley was at an all time high. My property had appreciated twenty percent in the last year. Not one to miss a God-given opportunity I realized this would give me the necessary funds to move. To leave the security of my home was another matter. I first realized I would need another doctor, and another good one. I discussed the idea with my doctor who seemed to imply there were no limits to what I could do, if I did so carefully.

There was a time when I came to peace about this decision. I would simply take it step by step: I would first find a job, then find a house, leave a job, sell a house, and drive across the country with my cat.

Realizing that I could not take on all the stress of a new hospital job at the same time I moved, I first sought another nursing home position. There was a tremendous need for registered nurses in the community I was moving to, and I didn't have any trouble finding a position.

I had to jump through hoops to get a license in another state, but I was prepared for this. I had to provide documentation and expunge a former misdemeanor. At each step I admit to being fearful something would prevent my decision. But everything seemed to come together at the last minute despite the odds.

Appropriately enough, I arrived in my new hometown on Thanksgiving. I moved into my new home the next week and started another position within a few days.

After three months of employment at the nursing home I made the decision to find a job at the nearby hospital. I interviewed for more than one position, but the one that seemed dearest to my heart was the one that I chose. I found a position as a registered nurse on a rehabilitation unit for brain injuries.

Wholeness

There are no two identical cases of bipolar illness any more than there are any two precisely identical people. My definition of wholeness would have to come from the mission statement at my current workplace: to see life beyond disability. This is not the same as seeing life *without* the disability. To see without the disability would imply denial of the illness. My life is constant attention to the small detail, and that is how I stay healthy.

I am writing this after a manic spree that was without incident. I did not get fired at work, drain my savings account, or make radical changes on impulse. I recognized the potential to do all of this and more, and my fear, healthy fear, prevented more than a low grade episode. I have recognized that it is not good for me to be alone since other people act as the barometers of my moods. I can see when my laugh is so loud that it scares someone, when my reaction is out of proportion to the event, and when my activity is beyond the limits of healthy. To get such feedback, I have stayed plugged into my workplace, my church, and my community.

As life is a dichotomy, the flip side of this precise attention to detail is that I do not spend every waking moment taking the pulse of each mood. I can be happy or sad just like anyone else. To recognize when the good or bad feelings are out of proportion to what might be considered normal is the essential skill I have acquired. My good doctors have put me in the driver's seat and, because it took me a long time to get here, I drive very carefully.

I must admit that, frequently, and for weeks at a time, I completely forget that I have the illness. It is a bit like driving and not paying attention until a light on the dashboard starts blinking. It may be inconvenient to pull off the road and get service, but unless one has developed the discipline to do so, one should not be driving.

I am very careful to whom I reveal the details of my condition as I do not want to be defined by it. I am angered every time a suicidal killer is defined by bipolar illness in the news. We don't define killers by the presence of heart disease or any other medical condition so why do we define them by mental illness? Upon learning of my illness casual acquaintances usually respond with one of two reactions. Either, they do not believe I was ever as sick as I once was, or they believe that I will not have the condition in the future once I have "straightened out the details of my life." My need for a very balanced life is rarely respected, and I have to fight to attain this balance. I am a bit like a unicycle rider on an uphill plank who has fallen off one too many times. There are few people I allow into my inner circle, and I have learned to choose them wisely.

Health is a journey and not a destination, and, as I am on my journey, my friends are on theirs. I do not have the right to wake them incessantly in the middle of the night, cry on their shoulders endlessly all day, or to always put my needs ahead of theirs. I do not have the right to constantly inconvenience my employer. I compensate for inevitable missed work with extra effort when I am present. I invest my money in a house payment so there is little available cash to spend on a spree, and I will have resources when I need them.

The flip side of all this is, at times, I do call friends in the middle of the night, cry on their shoulders, and put my needs ahead of theirs. I sometimes inconvenience my employer. I have spent money on something I wanted, whether or not it would be considered a spree. In short, I fail.

I have learned to forgive myself for failure, pick up my unique set of genes, and carry on.

Endnotes

1. Charles H. Spurgeon, Morning and Evening: A New Edition of the Classic Devotional Based on The Holy Bible, English Standard Version. Revised and updated by Alistair Begg. (Wheaton: Crossway Books, 2003).

2. Michael Hooper, "The Legacy of Menninger," The Topeka Capital-Journal, 4 May 2003.

3. Benedikt Amann and Heinz Grunze, "Neurochemical Underpinnings in Bipolar Disorder and Epilepsy," Epilepsia 46(Suppl. 4) 2005, (Munich: Blackwell Publishing, 2005). 26–30.

4. James Strong, LL.D., S.T.D., The New Strong's Exhaustive Concordance of the Bible (Nashville: Nelson Publishers, 1990), 54.